The Creative Curriculum® *for* Preschool

Teaching Guide
Getting Ready for Kindergarten

Heather Baker and Kai-leé Berke

TeachingStrategies® · Bethesda, MD

Copyright © 2015 by Teaching Strategies, LLC.

All rights reserved. No part of this text may be reproduced in any form or by any electronic or mechanical means, including information storage and retrieval systems, without prior written permission from Teaching Strategies, LLC, except in the case of brief quotations embodied in critical articles or reviews.

An exception is also made for the forms and the letters to families that are included in this guide. Permission is granted to duplicate those pages for use by the teachers/providers of the particular program that purchased these materials in order to implement The Creative Curriculum® for Preschool in the program. These materials may not be duplicated for training purposes without the express written permission of Teaching Strategies, LLC.

The publisher and the authors cannot be held responsible for injury, mishap, or damages incurred during the use of or because of the information in this book. The authors recommend appropriate and reasonable supervision at all times based on the age and capability of each child.

Editor: Kimberly Maxwell
Design and Layout: Jeff Cross, Abner Nieves
Spanish Translation: Aura Triana-Pacheco
Cover Design: Abner Nieves

Teaching Strategies, LLC
7101 Wisconsin Avenue, Suite 700
Bethesda, MD 20814

www.TeachingStrategies.com

978-1-60617-654-2

Teaching Strategies and Creative Curriculum names and logos are registered trademarks of, and GOLD and GOLDplus names are trademarks of, Teaching Strategies, LLC, Bethesda, MD. Brand-name products of other companies are suggested for illustrative purposes and are not required for implementation of the curriculum.

| 1 2 3 4 5 6 7 8 9 10 | 20 19 18 17 16 15 |
| Printing | Year Printed |

Printed and bound in the United States of America

Acknowledgments

We are grateful to Jo Wilson for her unparalleled organizational skills and sense of humor as she kept us on task and on time with our manuscripts.

Our editor, Kimberly Maxwell, patiently refined and polished our work, queried our intentions, and helped us get our message across in an approachable way.

Aura Triana provided Spanish translations for this Teaching Guide with skill and sensitivity—thank you so much, Aura, for enabling us to reach and engage more teachers and learners.

We would like to thank Clarissa Martínez for reviewing of the *Book Discussion Cards*™ and Holly Johnson for coordinating the printing. Thank you both for your thoughtfulness and dedication to this product.

Our gratitude and thanks are also expressed to Abner Nieves for designing the perfect cover for this book and to Jeff Cross for his impressive speed and attention to detail in helping us get the pages right.

Table of Contents

Getting Started

2   Introduction

3   Social–Emotional Considerations at the End of the Year

5   Preparing for the Last Few Weeks

6   A Letter to Families

Focus Questions

10   Focus Question 1
How is kindergarten like preschool? How is it different?
(Days 1–5)

22   Focus Question 2
How do we feel about going to kindergarten?
(Days 1–5)

34   Focus Question 3
How do we make and keep friends in kindergarten?
(Days 1–5)

Reflecting and Celebrating

50   Reflecting and Celebrating
(Days 1–5)

Resources

64   Children's Books

70   Teacher Resources

72   Weekly Planning Form

Getting Started

Getting Ready for Kindergarten Getting Started

Introduction

The end of the school year is an exciting time! This *Teaching Guide* contains a collection of daily plans that will help you prepare for the end of the preK year and the transition to kindergarten. During the last several weeks of the school year, you will be busy supporting children as they say good-bye to the familiarity of their classroom, their routines, and possibly even their friends, while also helping them look forward to moving on to kindergarten. By using the plans in this *Teaching Guide*, you will be able to continue to organize the day in the same way that you normally do while introducing the new ideas and experiences that come with the end of the preK year.

Some children may be familiar with kindergarten already because of older siblings who have gone through the transition or because there is a kindergarten in your school and they will simply be moving on to a new classroom down the hall. For other children, their transition may involve moving from a small, private preschool experience to a larger public elementary school. No matter the circumstances, expect that children may have questions about what lies ahead. We've chosen a few that are typical and used them to structure your classroom conversations and learning during the final four weeks of school.

For the last week, you'll find a collection of daily plans that you may use to help children reflect on and celebrate the learning that has taken place throughout the year. During this weeklong experience, you'll guide children through the process of reflecting on all they've learned, celebrating their achievements, and sharing their experiences with families and friends. It is important to take time to celebrate the school year. Even if you teach in a year-round program, pick a time to celebrate the end of the year. It is an important opportunity for the children and for you to reflect on your year together and to look forward to kindergarten.

Getting Ready for Kindergarten Getting Started

Social–Emotional Considerations at the End of the Year

Children often see school as an extension of home—where they belong, are loved, and are encouraged. Leaving this home can feel stressful or scary for children. Whether children are moving to a kindergarten classroom down the hall or to completely new schools, expect that many will experience strong emotions—fear, anxiety, extreme joy, excitement, sadness, or frustration. You may notice that these feelings impact their behavior in the classroom, and families may notice changes in behavior at home. It is important to remember that this is to be expected.

Throughout this *Teaching Guide*, you'll find strategies for supporting children's social–emotional development as they become comfortable with the transition from preK to kindergarten. This is also a great time to revisit some of your social–emotional *Intentional Teaching Cards*™ for guidance on supporting children and guiding their behavior in positive ways. Here is a list of *Intentional Teaching Cards*™ that you might find particularly useful during this time:

SE03 "Calm-Down Place" As children experience a range of emotions, it may help them to know that they have a quiet, calm place to visit in the classroom.

SE04 "Actively Listening to Children" This is a critical time in the school year for children to feel they are being heard and understood.

SE06 "Talk About Feelings" Specific guidance is included for using this card in the daily plans, but it can be useful any time to help children find the words for their feelings.

SE10 "My Turn at the Microphone" Giving children the chance to speak freely and listen to their peers may allow them the opportunity to express feelings and concerns they might not otherwise discuss.

SE17 "Supporting Children to Use Their Words" It's important for children to feel that they're being heard. To help them be effective communicators, you can guide them to express themselves and what they're feeling.

SE18 "Encouragement" So much is changing at this time of the year. It's great for children to be reminded of what they can do, and not just what will be new and strange as they transition to kindergarten.

The time you invest now in supporting children's social–emotional development will prepare them for the transition to kindergarten and help them find their place in an elementary school environment.

> **Read more about guidelines for planning for supporting children's social–emotional needs and guiding their behaviors in positive ways in *The Creative Curriculum*® *for Preschool, Volume 1: The Foundation*, Chapter 4.**

Families, too, may have conflicting emotions during this time. In the same way that partnerships with families were a critical part of children's smooth transition into your program, family partnerships at the end of the year are vital to the successful shift of children becoming kindergarten students. As you approach the end of the school year, take time to talk with families about their concerns and questions.

The Creative Curriculum® *for Preschool*

3

Getting Ready for Kindergarten Getting Started

Consider the following strategies for supporting families this time of year:

Conduct a transition conference with each family, during which you can talk about children's learning and development and how much they've grown over the year. This is also a good time to address any concerns families may have about "academics" in kindergarten.

Gather information about the schools that children will attend, and learn what you can about those schools so that you can closely relate your classroom experiences to those in children's new kindergarten programs.

Talk with families about possible changes in behavior they may notice in their children during this time. Offer strategies for helping children manage stress, and provide as much consistency as possible between home and school so that children and families can take comfort in knowing what comes next for the remainder of the year.

If possible, connect families new to the kindergarten experience with alumni families who have already been through the transition.

Prepare transition materials for children and families. These can include summer reading suggestions, community events, or games and activities to do at home.

As you think about how to best support children and families during this time, it's important to reflect on your own feelings about the end of the school year. Just as children may experience anxiety, excitement, and sadness, teachers often feel these same emotions about the end of preK. *Have I prepared my children for kindergarten? How can I make their transition as easy as possible? What if I'm feeling sad and anxious?* These are all very common feelings and questions to have at this stressful time of year. You, the children in your class, and their families may all be excited as you look forward, sad about saying good-bye, and nervous about what's coming next. That's a lot to handle in the final weeks of school!

Take some time to reflect on the great work you've done together this year and how the experiences you've provided have prepared the children well for the upcoming transition to kindergarten. Talk with colleagues about your year, and note what went well and what you might like to do differently next year. Try to savor the end of the school year, and be proud of your outstanding teaching accomplishments!

Getting Ready for Kindergarten Getting Started

Preparing for the Last Few Weeks

Planning carefully for the final days of school can ease transitions and help children feel more comfortable and secure. You have spent an entire school year with these children, and you know how to best guide them. If you can anticipate their needs, you'll be better prepared to plan for their transition from preK and support them as they look forward to kindergarten. Remember that your personal connection with each child is the most valuable support tool you have during this time.

As you plan for the upcoming weeks, remember to keep the majority of your experiences consistent and familiar. Consistent routines help children feel more secure and will support their growing independence as they look ahead to new experiences. Children depend on the structure and routine of the school day. Your classroom rituals, which may seem like a small part of the school day, are important shared experiences that have special meaning to the children in your class. At the end of the year, these routines and rituals become even more important as children are asked to examine their feelings about the changes ahead. Continue to make your classroom routines nurturing experiences. For example, take an extra minute when meeting as a group at the beginning of the day to ask children how they're feeling, or give an extra hug at the end of the day as children make their way home. Encourage families to keep up with their family routines and rituals even as schedules change and new experiences are planned.

Visiting a kindergarten classroom can be a powerful experience to help ease any anxiety children may have and build excitement about the change. Many kindergartens have programs where children can visit their new school, ride the bus, meet their teacher, play on the playground, or eat lunch in the cafeteria. Building a strong relationship with the school administration is essential to positive transitions. The more familiar parents and teachers are with the kindergarten staff, the more comfortable the transition will be. Take time to familiarize yourself with the community kindergarten options and possibilities for the families in your programs.

This guide includes additional ideas to support children and families during the transition. Remember, time spent in planning and preparing for the last days of the school year will help make the transition smooth and help children feel ready to ease into their new school environment. Review the daily plans included in this *Teaching Guide*. Begin gathering materials needed for choice time and small-group experiences. Read the "Reflecting and Celebrating" section of this *Teaching Guide* and make decisions about how best to celebrate children's accomplishments this year. Browse through the social–emotional section of your *Intentional Teaching Cards™*. These cards will be very helpful when supporting children as they prepare for their next steps as students.

Transitions can be hard and exciting. With planning, sensitivity, and a positive attitude, they can provide children and their families with a tremendous sense of accomplishment and confidence. Congratulations on a successful school year!

The Creative Curriculum® for Preschool

Getting Ready for Kindergarten Getting Started

A Letter to Families

Send families a letter explaining the focus of the final four weeks of school. Use the letter to communicate with families and as an opportunity to invite their participation during this time.

Dear Families,

Many of us have fond memories of kindergarten. What we might not remember is the anxiety and excitement we may have felt leading up to our entry into elementary school. The final weeks of school can be scary, fun, and exciting all at the same time, and not just for children! It's understandable for you to experience a range of emotions about your child moving from preK to kindergarten.

When children go through big life changes, such as the transition from preschool to elementary school, they may have big feelings that they aren't able to easily communicate. In our program, we welcome you to come and talk to us about how to support children at home and ease any anxiety they may feel. We know that this is an important milestone in your child's life. We are here to support your family.

If possible, we would love for you to share photos of family members in kindergarten for us to display in our classroom. Please label all photos with your name so we can return them at the end of the year. We promise to take good care of them!

What You Can Do at Home

Acknowledge your child's feelings. Know that some behaviors may be because of anxiety about the transition.

Keep your home routines and rituals consistent. This will help your child feel a sense of security and stability at home.

Read books about moving on to kindergarten, and talk with your child about the characters and their feelings.

Encourage older siblings to share their kindergarten experiences, and share your own fond memories.

Learn what you can in advance about your child's kindergarten teacher, classroom, and routines. If possible, visit the kindergarten class before the start of the school year. With your child, write down any questions you have for the teacher or school staff.

Talk with families of children who already attend the school. Ask them questions about their experiences and for any advice they have for new families.

We look forward to seeing you at the end-of-year celebration!

Getting Ready for Kindergarten Getting Started

Carta a las familias

Envíeles a las familias una carta para explicarles en qué se centran las cuatro últimas semanas del año. Utilice la carta para comunicarse con las familias y como oportunidad para invitarlas a participar durante ese periodo.

Apreciadas familias:

Muchos de nosotros tenemos recuerdos gratos del kindergarten. Pero es posible que no recordemos la ansiedad y la emoción que hayamos sentido cuando se aproximaba la fecha de entrar a la primaria. Las semanas finales del año pueden entusiasmar, divertir y causar temor al mismo tiempo, y no solo a los niños. Es comprensible que ustedes tengan distintas emociones sobre el paso de su niño del preescolar al kindergarten.

Cuando los niños pasan por cambios importantes en su vida, como la transición del preescolar a la primaria, pueden tener sentimientos fuertes que no pueden comunicar con facilidad. Los invitamos a acudir a nuestro programa a conversar sobre cómo apoyar a su niño en el hogar y calmar la ansiedad que pueda sentir. Sabemos que este es un hito importante en la vida de su niño. Aquí estamos para apoyar a su familia.

Si es posible, nos gustaría que trajeran fotos de otros miembros de la familia en el kindergarten para exhibirlas en el salón. Escriban su nombre al reverso de todas las fotos para que se las podamos devolver al final del año. ¡Les prometemos cuidarlas!

Qué puede hacer en el hogar

Acepten las emociones de su niño. Sepan que algunas conductas pueden deberse a la ansiedad sobre la transición.

Mantengan sus rutinas y ritos habituales. Eso le dará a su niño la sensación de que su hogar es seguro y estable.

Lean libros sobre el paso al kindergarten y hablen con el niño sobre los personajes y sus emociones.

Pídanles a los hermanos mayores que hablen de sus experiencias en el kindergarten y mencionen sus propios recuerdos gratos.

Averigüen lo que puedan sobre el maestro de kindergarten de su niño, su salón y las rutinas. Si pueden, visiten la clase antes de que comience el año. Escriban con su niño las preguntas que tengan para el maestro o el personal de la escuela.

Hablen con las familias de otros niños que asisten a la escuela. Pregúntenles sobre sus experiencias y pídanles consejos para las familias nuevas.

¡Esperamos verlos en nuestra celebración de fin de año!

The Creative Curriculum® for Preschool

Focus Questions

| | | AT A GLANCE | # Focus Question 1 |

How is kindergarten like preschool? How is it different?

Vocabulary—English: *kindergarten, prediction, school subject, anticipate*

	Day 1	Day 2	Day 3
Interest Areas	Library: photos of kindergarten classrooms	Library: chart from large group; writing materials	Blocks: photos of kindergarten classrooms
Question of the Day	Which of these looks like a classroom? (Display a few pictures: one of an elementary school classroom and two other rooms that are very different, e.g., restaurant, post office, doctor's office, etc.)	Which of these is one of our classroom rules? (List three things, one classroom rule and two other statements, e.g., wear your coat inside all day, leave the toys on the floor when you're finished, etc.)	How many syllables are in the word *kindergarten*?
Large Group	**Movement:** Clap the Beat **Discussion and Shared Writing:** What Do We Know About Kindergarten? **Materials:** Mighty Minutes 59, "Clap the Beat"; a collection of photos of kindergarten classrooms	**Rhyme:** Are You Ready? **Discussion and Shared Writing:** Planning for a Site Visit **Materials:** Mighty Minutes 73, "Are You Ready?"; chart paper for site visit predictions	**Game:** Thumbs Up **Discussion and Shared Writing:** Preparing for Our Site Visit **Materials:** Mighty Minutes 33, "Thumbs Up"; list of site visit predictions
Read-Aloud	Selection of a fiction book from the "Children's Books" list	*Get Set! Swim!* Book Discussion Card 41 (first read-aloud)	Selection of a fiction book from the "Children's Books" list
Small Group	**Option 1: What's Missing?** Intentional Teaching Card LL18, "What's Missing?"; collection of familiar classroom objects; bag or box; large piece of paper or cardboard **Option 2: Memory Games** Intentional Teaching Card LL08, "Memory Games"; set of memory cards that reflect common items found in the classroom	**Option 1: Dinnertime** Intentional Teaching Card M01, "Dinnertime"; paper or plastic dishes; utensils; napkins; cups; placemats **Option 2: Let's Go Fishing** Intentional Teaching Card M39, "Let's Go Fishing"; child-sized fishing poles made from a stick or dowel, string, and a magnet; set of fish cards; paper clips	**Option 1: Same/Different Book** Intentional Teaching Card LL04, "Bookmaking"; cardboard or card stock; paper; pencils, crayons, or markers; bookbinding supplies; clipboards **Option 2: Same/Different Computer Book** Intentional Teaching Card LL02, "Desktop Publishing"; digital camera; computer; each child's word bank; printer; paper; bookbinding supplies
Mighty Minutes™	Mighty Minutes 20, "I Can Make a Circle"	Mighty Minutes 50, "1, 2, 3, What Do I See?"	Mighty Minutes 75, "Busy Bees"

Spanish: *kindergarten, predicción, asignatura, esperar*

Day 4	Day 5	Make Time for…
Toys and Games: memory matching games	Library: fiction and nonfiction books about going to kindergarten	## Outdoor Experiences
Which of these is different? (Display three similar objects and one that is different, e.g., three different mittens and one glove, or three hardcover books and one paperback.)	How are these the same? (Display three objects that have a common characteristic, e.g., a marble, a beach ball, and an orange.)	**Physical Fun** • Review Intentional Teaching Card P16, "Body Part Balance." Follow the guidance on the card. ## Family Partnerships
Poem: "High in the Tree" **Discussion and Shared Writing:** What Is Different About Kindergarten? **Materials:** Mighty Minutes 51, "High in the Tree"; chart paper for "What Is Different About Kindergarten?" chart	Game: I Spy With My Little Eye **Discussion and Shared Writing:** What Is the Same About Kindergarten? **Materials:** Mighty Minutes 19, "I Spy With My Little Eye"; chart paper for "What Is the Same About Kindergarten?" chart	• Send families the letter at the beginning of the *Teaching Guide* that explains the end-of-year experience. • Invite families to assist with supervision during the visit to a kindergarten classroom. • Invite families to send in photos of family members in kindergarten.
Get Set! Swim! Book Discussion Card 41 (second read-aloud)	Selection of a poetry book from the "Children's Books" list	## Wow! Experiences • Day 3: Visit to a kindergarten classroom
Option 1: Same/Different Book Intentional Teaching Card LL04, "Bookmaking"; cardboard or card stock; paper; pencils, crayons, or markers; bookbinding supplies; clipboards **Option 2: Same/Different Computer Book** Intentional Teaching Card LL02, "Desktop Publishing"; digital camera; computer; each child's word bank; printer; paper; bookbinding supplies	Option 1: Observing Changes Intentional Teaching Card M07, "Ice Cubes"; ice cubes; paper towels; cups; measuring tools **Option 2: Baggie Ice Cream** Intentional Teaching Card M08, "Baggie Ice Cream" (See card for equipment, ingredients, and recipe.)	**Arrange to visit a kindergarten classroom and another special room in the school, such as the cafeteria, gymnasium, or library.** **Invite families to visit the class at any point over the next four weeks to talk about their kindergarten memories.**
Mighty Minutes 18, "I'm Thinking Of…"	Mighty Minutes 64, "Paper Towel Rap"; a paper towel roll for each child	

Day 1 Focus Question 1

How is kindergarten like preschool? How is it different?

Vocabulary
English: *kindergarten*
Spanish: *kindergarten*

Question of the Day: Which of these looks like a classroom? (Display a few pictures: one of an elementary school classroom and two other rooms that are very different, e.g., restaurant, post office, doctor's office waiting room, etc.)

Large Group

Opening Routine

- Sing a welcome song and talk about who's here.

Movement: Clap the Beat

- Use Mighty Minutes 59, "Clap the Beat."
- Follow the guidance on the card. Include the word *kindergarten,* and talk about how many syllables are in the word.

Discussion and Shared Writing: What Do We Know About Kindergarten?

- Review the question of the day. Encourage children to talk about the characteristics of the classroom in the picture.
- Explain, "I brought a few pictures to share with you from a kindergarten classroom I visited. Kindergarten is the new class you will go to when you are finished with preschool."
- Show children the photos of the kindergarten classroom you visited. If you have photos of multiple classrooms, display a few from each class.

- Say, "There are so many things to discover about kindergarten. Let's look at these photos and see what we find."
- Invite children to examine the photos and point out familiar objects.
- If there are unfamiliar items in the photos, ask, "What do you think this is?"
- Record children's ideas about both familiar and unfamiliar items.
- Ask, "Has anyone here been to a kindergarten classroom before? What did you see?"
- Add any additional responses to the list of items.

Before transitioning to interest areas, point out that the collection of photos of the kindergarten classroom will be available in the Library area for the children to explore or bring to other areas.

Getting Ready for Kindergarten Focus Questions

Choice Time

As you interact with children in the interest areas, make time to do the following:

- Explore the photos of the kindergarten classroom with the children.

- Pay attention to what children know about kindergarten, what they find interesting, and what questions they ask. Record their ideas.

- Ask open-ended questions that encourage children to talk about their future kindergarten experiences. For example, "This picture shows a group of children playing basketball. What do you think you would play with on this playground?"

> **Observe children for signs of distress when talking about new experiences. For children who are wary of change, introduce new ideas slowly and give them plenty of time to adjust. See Intentional Teaching Card SE04, "Actively Listening to Children," for additional strategies.**

Read-Aloud

Choose a storybook from the "Children's Books" list found on pages 64–69. See the accompanying guidance for ideas about sharing the book with children.

Small Group

Option 1: What's Missing?

- Review Intentional Teaching Card LL18, "What's Missing?" Follow the guidance on the card.

- Include a collection of familiar classroom objects.

Option 2: Memory Games

- Review Intentional Teaching Card LL08, "Memory Games." Follow the guidance on the card.

- Create memory cards that reflect common items found in the classroom. As you play, talk about which items might also be found in a kindergarten classroom.

Mighty Minutes™

- Use Mighty Minutes 20, "I Can Make a Circle." Follow the guidance on the card.

Large-Group Roundup

- Recall the day's events.

- Choose one photo from the collection of kindergarten classroom photos. Invite children who explored the photos to talk about what they noticed.

The Creative Curriculum® for Preschool

13

Day 2 Focus Question 1

How is kindergarten like preschool? How is it different?

Vocabulary
English: *prediction*; See Book Discussion Card 41, *Get Set! Swim!*, for additional words
Spanish: *predicción*

Question of the Day: Which of these is one of our classroom rules? (List three things, one classroom rule and two other statements, e.g., wear your coat inside all day, leave the toys on the floor when you're finished, etc.)

Large Group

Opening Routine

- Sing a welcome song and talk about who's here.

Rhyme: Are You Ready?

- Use Mighty Minutes 73, "Are You Ready?" Follow the guidance of the second bullet on the back of the card.

Discussion and Shared Writing: Planning for a Site Visit

- Explain, "Tomorrow we'll be visiting a kindergarten classroom. Not all classrooms are the same, but this visit will show you what your kindergarten classroom might be like."

- Ask, "Can you think of any questions you have about the kindergarten classroom? We can write them down here." Chart children's responses.

- Say, "I wonder what we'll see in the kindergarten classroom. We can make *predictions* about what we'll see. When you make a prediction, you say what you think will happen. Our predictions will be about what we'll see in the kindergarten classroom tomorrow."

- Invite children to make predictions about the classroom. Offer assistance as needed by wondering aloud. For example, "I wonder if the classroom we visit will have a class pet."

- Save the list of predictions and questions for later reference.

Before transitioning to interest areas, explain that the list of predictions and questions will be available in the Library area so that children can make more predictions and add them to the list.

Getting Ready for Kindergarten Focus Questions

Choice Time

As you interact with children in the interest areas, make time to do the following:

- Review the question of the day.

- Talk with children about what they think the rules might be in kindergarten. Wonder aloud about your classroom rules and other rules they might learn. For example, "We have a rule about putting materials away when we are finished using them. I wonder if the classroom we visit tomorrow has a rule like that."

- Ask open-ended questions that encourage them to make other predictions. For example, "What games do you think children play in kindergarten? Where do you think they eat their lunch?"

- Record any predictions and questions children ask.

Read-Aloud

Read *Get Set! Swim!*

- Use Book Discussion Card 41, *Get Set! Swim!* Follow the guidance for the first read-aloud.

Small Group

Option 1: Dinnertime

- Review Intentional Teaching Card M01, "Dinnertime." Follow the guidance on the card.

Option 2: Let's Go Fishing

- Review Intentional Teaching Card M39, "Let's Go Fishing." Follow the guidance on the card.

Mighty Minutes™

- Use Mighty Minutes 50, "1, 2, 3, What Do I See?" Follow the guidance on the card.

Large-Group Roundup

- Recall the day's events.

- Remind children that tomorrow will include a visit to a kindergarten classroom.

- Review the list of predictions and questions for the site visit, and write down any additional questions or comments.

> As families send in photos of themselves in kindergarten, start a display in the classroom and discuss them with children.

The Creative Curriculum® for Preschool

15

Day 3 Focus Question 1

How is kindergarten like preschool? How is it different?

Vocabulary
English: *school subject*
Spanish: *asignatura*
Question of the Day: How many syllables are in the word *kindergarten*?

Large Group

Opening Routine
- Sing a welcome song and talk about who's here.

Game: Thumbs Up
- Use Mighty Minutes 33, "Thumbs Up." Follow the guidance on the back of the card that includes alliteration.

Discussion and Shared Writing: Preparing for Our Site Visit
- Review the question of the day. Explain, "Today we will be visiting a kindergarten classroom. We will be able to compare our classroom to the one we visit, and we can look for things that are the same and things that are different."
- Ask children to share any new ideas about their predictions. Review the list from yesterday and add to it as needed.
- Remind the children of your expectations for their behavior, e.g., stay together as a group; keep your hands to yourself unless an adult invites you to touch something.
- Take photos during the visit so children can later refer to the pictures.
- After the visit, review what children observed. Talk about any additional rooms they visited, and introduce any special *school subjects* that children may have in kindergarten. Define school subject as something to learn more about. For example, "I saw that the kindergarten class goes to the art room to learn about art. I wonder what other special rooms they visit."

Before transitioning to interest areas, talk about how children can use the photos of kindergarten classrooms to guide them in their creations in the Block area.

Getting Ready for Kindergarten Focus Questions

Choice Time

As you interact with children in the interest areas, make time to do the following:

- Listen for how children talk about what they see in the photos.

- Describe children's block creations as you interact with children. For example, "I see that you are making a desk for the teacher. That looks like the desk in this picture."

- Take pictures of children's block structures and display them next to the photos of the kindergarten classrooms.

Read-Aloud

Choose a storybook from the "Children's Books" list found on pages 64–69. See the accompanying guidance for additional ideas when sharing the book with children.

Small Group

Option 1: Same/Different Book

- Review Intentional Teaching Card LL04, "Bookmaking." Follow the guidance on the card.

- Invite children to create a book about the similarities and differences between your classroom and the kindergarten classroom they visited.

Option 2: Same/Different Computer Book

- Review Intentional Teaching Card LL02, "Desktop Publishing." Follow the guidance on the card.

- Invite children to create a book about the similarities and differences between your classroom and the kindergarten classroom they visited.

> Providing a digital camera for children to take their own pictures gives them more ownership over the bookmaking process. Invite them to use their own photos and the photos you took of the kindergarten classroom they visited.

Mighty Minutes™

- Use Mighty Minutes 75, "Busy Bees." Follow the guidance on the back of the card.

Large-Group Roundup

- Recall the day's events. Review the list of predictions and talk about the information found on the site visit.

- Write a group thank-you note to the school staff that met with the children on the site visit. Invite children to sign their names and add drawings to the note.

The Creative Curriculum® for Preschool

17

Day 4 Focus Question 1

How is kindergarten like preschool? How is it different?

Vocabulary

English: See Book Discussion Card 41, *Get Set! Swim!*, for words.

Question of the Day: Which of these is different? (Display three similar objects and one that is different, e.g., three different mittens and one glove, or three hardcover books and one paperback.)

Large Group

Opening Routine

- Sing a welcome song and talk about who's here.

Poem: High in the Tree

- Use Mighty Minutes 51, "High in the Tree." Follow the guidance on the card.
- Repeat the activity using the guidance of the last bullet on the back of the card.

Discussion and Shared Writing: What Is Different About Kindergarten?

- Review the question of the day. Talk about the characteristics of the similar objects and the characteristics of the one object that is different.
- Lead a discussion about what children saw during the site visit yesterday. Focus on what was different in the kindergarten classroom and the other places you visited.
- Say, "I noticed that the children in the kindergarten classroom were all sitting at tables and writing. When do we all sit down at tables?"
- Ask open-ended questions that encourage children to remember and describe differences between the classrooms. For example, "What did we see in the kindergarten classroom that was different from what we have? You noticed that they have different class jobs. What jobs do they have in the kindergarten class we visited?"
- Record children's responses on a "What is different about kindergarten?" chart.

Before transitioning to interest areas, point out the matching games available for play in the Toys and Games area. See Intentional Teaching Card LL08, "Memory Games," for guidance on supporting children's learning when playing matching games.

Getting Ready for Kindergarten Focus Questions

Choice Time

As you interact with children in the interest areas, make time to do the following:

- Observe children as they play the memory game.

- Encourage them to describe the pictures they are matching. Help them make connections between the pictures, and talk about what is different. For example, "You turned over two faces, but they don't match. What's different about them? You're right, one face is wearing glasses and the other one isn't. What else do you see that's different?"

- When children are done playing, discuss the strategies they used to help them remember where to find the matching cards.

> **If you know the children in your preK class will be expected to follow very different routines when they get to kindergarten, take a few days to practice these before the end of the year to familiarize children with the concepts. For example, play games that allow children to practice raising their hands, lining up, and walking quietly in a hallway.**

Read-Aloud

Read *Get Set! Swim!*

- Use Book Discussion Card 41, *Get Set! Swim!* Follow the guidance for the second read-aloud.

Small Group

Option 1: Same/Different Book

- Review Intentional Teaching Card LL04, "Bookmaking." Follow the guidance on the card.

- Invite children to create a book about the similarities and differences between your classroom and the kindergarten classroom they visited.

Option 2: Same/Different Computer Book

- Review Intentional Teaching Card LL02, "Desktop Publishing." Follow the guidance on the card.

- Invite children to create a book about the similarities and differences between your classroom and the kindergarten classroom they visited.

Mighty Minutes™

- Use Mighty Minutes 18, "I'm Thinking Of..." Follow the guidance of the first bullet on the back of the card.

Large-Group Roundup

- Recall the day's events.

- Invite children who made books during small-group time to share their creations.

The Creative Curriculum® for Preschool

19

Day 5 Focus Question 1

How is kindergarten like preschool? How is it different?

Vocabulary
English: *anticipate*
Spanish: *esperar*
Question of the Day: How are these the same? (Display three objects that have a common characteristic, e.g., a marble, a beach ball, and an orange.)

Large Group

Opening Routine

- Sing a welcome song and talk about who's here.

Game: I Spy With My Little Eye

- Use Mighty Minutes 19, "I Spy With My Little Eye." Follow the guidance on the card, then play again and choose a variation on the back of the card.

Discussion and Shared Writing: What Is the Same About Kindergarten?

- Review the question of the day. Encourage the children to talk about the characteristics of the objects and how they are the same.
- Lead a discussion about what children saw during the site visit earlier in the week. Focus on what was similar between your classroom and the kindergarten classroom and other places you visited. Show them the photos that you took to help them remember.
- Say, "I saw a long shelf of books to read in the kindergarten classroom. It looked like our Library area here. I even saw a few of the same books!"
- Ask open-ended questions that encourage children to remember and describe what they noticed that was similar between the classrooms. For example, "What did we see in the classroom that was the same as what we have? You noticed that they have cubbies for their coats and bags. How is that the same as our room?"
- Record children's responses on a "What is the same about kindergarten?" chart.

Before transitioning to interest areas, remind children that there are books about going to kindergarten in the Library area for them to explore.

20

Getting Ready for Kindergarten Focus Questions

Choice Time

As you interact with children in the interest areas, make time to do the following:

- Talk with children about the books they're exploring in the Library area. Encourage them to point out objects or events in the story that are similar to your classroom or similar to the kindergarten classroom you visited.

- Ask children to think about what they will look forward to doing in kindergarten. Introduce the word *anticipate* during the discussion. For example, "What do you think you'll like to do in kindergarten? So, you are glad you will get to ride the bus to school. You anticipate that will be fun. That means you're waiting for it and expecting it to be fun."

- Record the children's ideas with an audio or video recorder to share with children and families at a later time.

English-language learners
Encourage children to use gestures as they communicate. Demonstrate how gestures can help clarify meaning.

Read-Aloud

Share a poetry book from the "Children's Books" list found on pages 64–69. See the accompanying guidance for additional ideas when sharing the book with children.

Small Group

Option 1: Ice Cubes

- Review Intentional Teaching Card M07, "Ice Cubes." Follow the guidance on the card.

Option 2: Baggie Ice Cream

- Review Intentional Teaching Card M08, "Baggie Ice Cream." Follow the guidance on the card.

Mighty Minutes™

- Use Mighty Minutes 64, "Paper Towel Rap." Follow the guidance on the card. Encourage children to recite familiar rhymes.

Large-Group Roundup

- Recall the day's events.

- Invite children to share the things they discovered that were the same about their classroom and the kindergarten classroom they visited. Ask children who explored books in the Library area during choice time to think of additional similarities they found in the books about kindergarten.

The Creative Curriculum® for Preschool

	AT A GLANCE	Focus Question 2

How do we feel about going to kindergarten?

Vocabulary—English: words that describe feelings (e.g., *uneasy, joyful, confident, timid, eager,* etc.), *realistic, adventure*

	Day 1	Day 2	Day 3
Interest Areas	Library: personal journal for each child; variety of writing tools Art: materials for drawing and writing	Library: books about going to kindergarten	Dramatic Play: props or puppets for storytelling
Question of the Day	How do you feel today?	Which book would you like to read? (Offer three choices of books about going to kindergarten.)	Have you ever felt nervous?
Large Group	Movement: Leaping Sounds Discussion and Shared Writing: Words For Our Feelings Materials: Mighty Minutes 17, "Leaping Sounds"; chart paper; book selection from the Children's Book Collection	Movement: The Wave Discussion and Shared Writing: Feelings About Kindergarten Materials: Mighty Minutes 34, "The Wave"; books from the question of the day; chart paper	Rhyme: Three Rowdy Children Discussion and Shared Writing: Feeling Nervous Materials: Mighty Minutes 53, "Three Rowdy Children"; familiar book about feelings; chart paper
Read-Aloud	*Get Set! Swim!* Book Discussion Card 41 (third read-aloud)	Selection of a poetry book from the "Children's Books" list	*The Upside Down Boy* Book Discussion Card 42 (first read-aloud)
Small Group	Option 1: Character Feelings Intentional Teaching Card SE05, "Character Feelings"; books that focus on the feelings of the main character Option 2: Feelings Intentional Teaching Card SE06, "Talk About Feelings"; pictures of people exhibiting different emotions or interacting in different ways; writing and drawing materials	Option 1: Where's the Beanbag? Intentional Teaching Card M56, "Where's the Beanbag?"; beanbags; basket or tub; masking tape Option 2: Stepping Stones Intentional Teaching Card M55, "Stepping Stones"; masking tape or chalk	Option 1: Writing Poems Intentional Teaching Card LL27, "Writing Poems"; paper and pencils; audio recorder Option 2: Writing Poems Intentional Teaching Card LL27, "Writing Poems"; paper and pencils; audio recorder; poems that describe different feelings
Mighty Minutes™	Mighty Minutes 20, "I Can Make a Circle"	Mighty Minutes 24, "Dinky Doo"	Mighty Minutes 15, "Say It, Show It"

Spanish: palabras que se usan para describir emociones (e.g., *intranquilo, alegre, seguro de sí mismo, asustadizo, entusiasta,* etc.), *realista, aventura*

Day 4	Day 5	Make Time for…
Dramatic Play: props or puppets for storytelling	**Music and Movement:** recordings of lively music	## Outdoor Experiences **Physical Fun** • Review Intentional Teaching Card P12, "Exploring Pathways." Follow the guidance on the card. ## Family Partnerships • Invite families to continue sharing photos of family members in kindergarten.
What comes next in the pattern? (Create a simple repeating pattern for children to extend.)	Which of these children look excited? (Display three different photos of children with different facial expressions or doing different actions.)	
Game: Let's Pretend **Discussion and Shared Writing:** Feeling Excited **Materials:** Mighty Minutes 39, "Let's Pretend"; new materials to introduce to the group; chart paper	**Song:** "My Body Jumps" **Discussion and Shared Writing:** How Do We Show Excitement? **Materials:** Mighty Minutes 72, "My Body Jumps"; chart paper	
Selection of a nonfiction book from the "Children's Books" list	*The Upside Down Boy* Book Discussion Card 42 (second read-aloud)	
Option 1: Action Patterns Intentional Teaching Card M35, "Action Patterns"; action cards; pocket chart **Option 2: Picture Patterns** Intentional Teaching Card M45, "Picture Patterns"; a collection of photos of familiar classroom objects with patterns; digital camera; paper and writing materials; collage materials	**Option 1: Storyboard** Intentional Teaching Card LL46, "Storyboard"; images from question of the day; tape; construction paper; writing tools **Option 2: Kindergarten Story** Intentional Teaching Card LL46, "Storyboard"; images from question of the day and site visit; tape; construction paper; writing tools	
Mighty Minutes 88, "Disappearing Rhymes"	Mighty Minutes 03, "Purple Pants"	

23

Day 1 Focus Question 2

How do we feel about going to kindergarten?

Vocabulary

English: words to describe feelings such as *uneasy, joyful, confident, timid, eager*; See Book Discussion Card 41, *Get Set! Swim!*, for additional words.

Spanish: palabras con las cuales se describen las emociones, *como intranquilo, alegre, seguro de sí mismo, asustadizo, entusiasta*

Question of the Day: How do you feel today?

Large Group

Opening Routine

- Sing a welcome song and talk about who's here.

Movement: Leaping Sounds

- Use Mighty Minutes 17, "Leaping Sounds." Follow the guidance on the back of the card, using the ending sounds of children's names.

Discussion and Shared Writing: Words for Our Feelings

- Review the question of the day. If children use basic feeling words such as *happy, sad,* or *mad* to describe how they feel, introduce them to more complex words for those feelings, such as *content/delighted, moody/sorrowful,* or *furious/upset*.

- Choose a book from the Children's Book Collection that was featured in the *Beginning the Year Teaching Guide*, such as *Charlie Anderson, Too Many Tamales,* or *A Pocket for Corduroy*. Read the story, and as you read, invite children to talk about the feelings of the characters.

> See the accompanying *Book Discussion Card*, if applicable, for guidance to support children's understanding of the social–emotional concepts in the story.

- Encourage children to use some of their new words for feelings in the discussion. For example, "Nathan says that Charlie Anderson looks happy sleeping on the bed on this page. How else could we describe what he's feeling? We could say he looks content and satisfied."

- Invite children to share a memory of a time when they felt like the characters they describe. Record their responses.

Before transitioning to interest areas, explain, "Sometimes it can be hard to talk about how we feel, but it might be easier to draw or write about our feelings." Show them their journals or where they can find paper and pencils in the Library or Art areas.

Getting Ready for Kindergarten Focus Questions

Choice Time

> **See Intentional Teaching Card LL39, "My Daily Journal," for more information about interacting with children as they write and draw in their journals.**

As you interact with children in the interest areas, make time to do the following:

- Invite children to write or draw pictures to describe how they feel.

- Talk with them about their feelings. Reflect back to them what you see and hear. For example, "You're excited that it's your turn to feed our class pet today. You drew our fish, Oliver, and you sound thrilled when you talk about doing that job!"

- Record children's dictation about their drawings, as appropriate.

English-language learners
English-language learners and English-speaking children can benefit from interacting with each other during choice-time activities. Hearing their classmates use English as they talk about their feelings or draw pictures helps English-language learners develop oral language competency.

Read-Aloud

Read *Get Set! Swim!*

- Use Book Discussion Card 41, *Get Set! Swim!* Follow the guidance for the third read-aloud.

Small Group

Option 1: Character Feelings

- Review Intentional Teaching Card SE05, "Character Feelings." Follow the guidance on the card.

- Use a book that focuses on the feelings of the main character.

• Option 2: Feelings

- Review Intentional Teaching Card SE06, "Talk About Feelings." Follow the guidance on the card.

- Use pictures of people exhibiting different emotions or interacting in different ways. Invite children to write or draw about the feelings they observe in the photos.

Mighty Minutes™

- Use Mighty Minutes 20, "I Can Make a Circle."

- Follow the guidance on the back of the card and invite the children to work together in groups to create the shapes.

- Observe and record children's interactions. After the activity, talk about what you observed, and invite children to share their feelings about the experience.

Large-Group Roundup

- Recall the day's events. Reinforce the new vocabulary introduced during the day.

- Invite children who added to their journals to share their entries.

The Creative Curriculum® for Preschool

25

Day 2 Focus Question 2

How do we feel about going to kindergarten?

Vocabulary
English: *realistic*
Spanish: *realista*
Question of the Day: Which book would you like to read?
(Offer three choices of books about going to kindergarten.)

Large Group

Opening Routine

- Sing a welcome song and talk about who's here.

Movement: The Wave

- Use Mighty Minutes 34, "The Wave." Follow the guidance on the back of the card, inviting children to narrate the story and interpret how the waves move their bodies.

Discussion and Shared Writing: Feelings About Kindergarten

- Show children the three books about kindergarten from the question of the day.

- Talk about the question of the day. Tally the results together, and then read the book that got the most votes from the poll.

- As you read, pause to reflect back on what children learned about kindergarten from the site visit and compare it to information in the book. For example, "In this story, it looks like Emily rides a bus to school. The students we visited also ride the bus. I like the color of this bus. It's bright yellow."

- Point out the feelings and feeling words used in the story to describe the characters' experiences in a new school. For example, "Look how she's holding her teddy bear so tightly. How do you think she feels about her first day in kindergarten?"

- After reading, invite children to share their own feelings about the story and the characters' experiences. Record their responses, and save the list for later reference.

Before transitioning to interest areas, explain that the book you just read and other books about going to kindergarten will be available in the Library area for children to explore.

Getting Ready for Kindergarten Focus Questions

Choice Time

As you interact with children in the interest areas, make time to do the following:

- Observe children as they explore the books about going to kindergarten.

- Encourage children to think about what they know from their kindergarten visit. Introduce the word *realistic*, and ask children to think about how realistic the depictions might be in the books. For example, "In this book, Tim is going to meet his new teacher and see his classroom. He thinks everything will be big and scary, but then he sees all of the fun things there are to do. Do you think his classroom looks realistic? That means it looks real. I think so, too. It looks similar to the class we visited."

- Invite children to make comparisons between the characters and experiences in the books. Refer to the list of responses from earlier in the day, and talk with children about their own feelings and the feelings of the characters. Record their responses.

Read-Aloud

Choose a poetry book from the "Children's Books" list found on pages 64–69. See the accompanying guidance for ideas about sharing the book with children.

Small Group

Option 1: Where's the Beanbag?

- Review Intentional Teaching Card M56, "Where's the Beanbag?" Follow the guidance on the card.

Option 2: Stepping Stones

- Review Intentional Teaching Card M55, "Stepping Stones." Follow the guidance on the card.

English-language learners
Teacher-guided small-group activities offer opportunities for all children to get involved and interact with others. For children who typically work in isolation, the small-group structure is a good stepping stone to participation in a larger group.

Mighty Minutes™

- Use Mighty Minutes 24, "Dinky Doo." Follow the guidance on the back of the card, using letter cards.

Large-Group Roundup

- Recall the day's events.

- Invite children who explored the books about kindergarten to share their findings. Encourage them to explain the comparisons they made between the stories.

The Creative Curriculum® for Preschool

27

Day 3 Focus Question 2

How do we feel about going to kindergarten?

Vocabulary
English: *timid;* See Book Discussion Card 42, *The Upside Down Boy,* for words.
Spanish: *asustadizo*
Question of the Day: Have you ever felt nervous?

Large Group

Opening Routine
- Sing a welcome song and talk about who's here.

Rhyme: Three Rowdy Children
- Use Mighty Minutes 53, "Three Rowdy Children." Follow the guidance on the card, emphasizing the rhyming words.
- Use the variation on the back of the card, and encourage children to think of other words to describe the children in the rhyme, e.g., excited, sleepy, or scared.

Discussion and Shared Writing: Feeling Nervous
- Review the question of the day. Share an experience with children from a time when you felt nervous. For example, "Sometimes we feel nervous when we're trying something new. I remember that I felt nervous the first time I drove a car. I had learned all about driving, but I still felt nervous because I had never done it before. Can you think of a time when you felt nervous?" Record children's responses.
- Ask children to think about the new things they've learned about kindergarten. Invite them to share anything about kindergarten that they remember from the visit, and to talk about how it makes them feel. For example, "Kira said that she saw bigger tables and chairs in the classroom we visited, and she feels scared. I think seeing those bigger things might make someone nervous and anxious about going to kindergarten."
- Lead children in a picture walk of a familiar book about feelings, such as *Wemberly Worried*. Relate the characters' feelings to what children have shared during the discussion. For example, "We read this book at the beginning of the year when our class was new to you. Wemberly feels timid when she goes to school for the first time. Some of you described feeling *timid*, too. Timid means feeling scared and not very brave."

> When asking children to think about and talk about their feelings, be sure to allow plenty of time for them to reflect and respond.

Before transitioning to interest areas, explain to children that they can use the props or puppets in the Dramatic Play area to share stories with each other about a time when they felt nervous.

28

Getting Ready for Kindergarten Focus Questions

Choice Time

As you interact with children in the interest areas, make time to do the following:

- Observe children and record their storytelling experiences.

- Ask open-ended questions that prompt them to recall additional details and feelings from their stories.

- Use descriptive language to reflect their experiences back to them. For example, "It sounds like you were really nervous around that big dog. Your brother was helpful when he showed you how to ask the owner if the dog was friendly."

> When listening to children talk about their feelings, remember that their feelings, even about past experiences, are very real to them. Refrain from comments like, "That's silly," or "You didn't need to be scared." Instead, validate their feelings by reflecting them back to children.

Read-Aloud

Read *The Upside Down Boy*.

- Use Book Discussion Card 42, *The Upside Down Boy*. Follow the guidance for the first read-aloud.

English-language learners
When reading a book with text in English and another language, introduce the book and its important concepts in the home languages of English-language learners before you present and read the book aloud in English.

Small Group

Option 1: Writing Poems

- Review Intentional Teaching Card LL27, "Writing Poems." Follow the guidance on the card.

Option 2: Writing Poems

- Review Intentional Teaching Card LL27, "Writing Poems." Follow the guidance on the card.

- Share additional poems with children that describe different feelings.

Mighty Minutes™

- Use Mighty Minutes 15, "Say It, Show It." Follow the guidance on the back of the card.

Large-Group Roundup

- Recall the day's events.

- Invite children who told stories during choice time to share their experience. Encourage children to make comparisons between their stories and the stories that you've read recently about going to kindergarten.

The Creative Curriculum® for Preschool

29

Day 4　Focus Question 2

How do we feel about going to kindergarten?

Vocabulary

English: *adventure*
Spanish: *aventura*

Question of the Day: What comes next in the pattern?
(Create a simple repeating pattern for children to extend.)

Large Group

Opening Routine

- Sing a welcome song and talk about who's here.

Game: Let's Pretend

- Use Mighty Minutes 39, "Let's Pretend." Follow the guidance on the back of the card, inviting children to mimic different kinds of animals.

Discussion and Shared Writing: Feeling Excited

- Introduce one or two new materials to the group that can be used in an interest area or outdoors.

- Explain the new materials and talk about the excitement of doing something new. For example, "I'm so excited to be at school today because I brought something new for us to use in our classroom. It's a round tray that spins. Let's think about different ways we could use it."

- Restate and record children's responses. For example, "Yes, we could use it to make it easier for everyone to reach the bowl of snacks when we eat, or we could use it to display our clay creations. What else could we use it for? Could we use it outside?"

- Observe and reflect the excitement that children show about the new ideas. For example, "You sound very excited about using it in the Art area. We could tape paper to it and let it spin while we paint. I wonder what our paintings would look like if the paper is spinning."

- Talk about how it can be exciting to have an *adventure*, or an exciting and new experience, even if you don't always know what the outcome will be.

Before transitioning to interest areas, invite children to use the new materials in a particular interest area. Refer to the list of responses to decide on how to first use the items. Explain that they can also use the props or puppets in the Dramatic Play area to tell stories about a time when they were excited to do something new.

Getting Ready for Kindergarten Focus Questions

Choice Time

As you interact with children in the interest areas, make time to do the following:

- Observe children and record their storytelling experiences.

- Ask open-ended questions that prompt them to recall additional details and feelings from their stories.

- Use descriptive language to reflect their experiences back to them. For example, "It sounds like you were excited when you met your new baby sister. You had a lot of new experiences when she came home!"

- Support children to make connections between their own exciting experiences and the experience of going to kindergarten. Give them plenty of time to think about how their feelings might be the same across different adventures.

> **Audio or video recordings can be useful ways to capture children's direct quotes as they come up with new ideas and work creatively. This information can be particularly helpful for gathering documentation on cognitive and language objectives and dimensions.**

Read-Aloud

Choose a nonfiction book from the "Children's Books" list found on pages 64–69. See the accompanying guidance for additional ideas when sharing the book with children.

Small Group

Option 1: Action Patterns

- Review Intentional Teaching Card M35, "Action Patterns." Follow the guidance on the card.

- Review the question of the day. Support children to create a new action pattern using the pattern from the question of the day as their guide.

Option 2: School Patterns

- Review the question of the day.

- Review Intentional Teaching Card M45, "Picture Patterns." Follow the guidance on the card, including images of familiar classroom objects that have a pattern, e.g., numbers on a calendar, stripes on a flag, tiles on the floor, etc.

Mighty Minutes™

- Use Mighty Minutes 88, "Disappearing Rhymes." Follow the guidance on the card.

Large-Group Roundup

- Recall the day's events.

- Invite children who used the new materials to explain what they did.

- Encourage children to think of new and exciting things they may encounter in kindergarten.

The Creative Curriculum® for Preschool

31

Day 5 Focus Question 2

How do we feel about going to kindergarten?

Vocabulary

English: See Book Discussion Card 42, *The Upside Down Boy*, for words.

Question of the Day: Which of these children look excited? (Display three different photos of children with different facial expressions or doing different actions.)

Large Group

Opening Routine

- Sing a welcome song and talk about who's here.

Song: "My Body Jumps"

- Use Mighty Minutes 72, "My Body Jumps." Follow the guidance on the back of the card.

Discussion and Shared Writing: How Do We Show Excitement?

- Talk with children about the different ways they moved their bodies as they sang, "My Body Jumps."
- Review the question of the day. Ask, "How do we move when we feel excited? How do we show someone we're excited?" Record children's responses.
- Say, "When we feel excited, we want to celebrate! We can do that in so many ways."
- Invite children to stand and demonstrate how they show excitement. Describe their actions. For example, "Remy, you are really excited! You are waving your arms in the air!" Record their words and actions.
- Say, "When we start kindergarten, we might feel nervous, and we might feel excited, too. In kindergarten, there will be lots of new and exciting adventures."
- Encourage children to think of other ways to show excitement, e.g., drawing a picture, wearing a brightly colored shirt, singing a lively song, etc.

Before transitioning to interest areas, explain that there will be peppy music to listen to in the Music and Movement area, and children can explore different ways to move to show excitement.

Getting Ready for Kindergarten Focus Questions

Choice Time

As you interact with children in the interest areas, make time to do the following:

- Listen for how children talk about the music they hear.

- Use descriptive language to describe how the music makes you feel and how you want to move to the music. For example, "This music with different kinds of drums makes me want to clap my hands. I feel joyful when I hear it."

- Ask open-ended questions that encourage children to think about how the music makes them feel and how they want to move.

English-language learners
When discussing emotions with English-language learners, act out the emotions or refer to images of children demonstrating the emotions to reinforce subtle differences.

Read-Aloud

Read *The Upside Down Boy*.

- Use Book Discussion Card 42, *The Upside Down Boy*. Follow the guidance for the second read-aloud.

Small Group

Option 1: Storyboard

- Review Intentional Teaching Card LL46, "Storyboard." Follow the guidance on the card. Use the images from the question of day.

Option 2: Kindergarten

- Review Intentional Teaching Card LL46, "Storyboard." Follow the guidance on the card. Use a variety of images including the images from the question of the day and photos from the kindergarten site visit.

Mighty Minutes™

- Use Mighty Minutes 03, "Purple Pants." Follow the guidance of the third bullet on the back of the card, emphasizing the beginning sounds of words.

Large-Group Roundup

- Recall the day's events.

- Invite children who created a storyboard to tell the story they created. Relate the story, if appropriate, to the experiences they may have in kindergarten.

The Creative Curriculum® for Preschool

33

	AT A GLANCE	**Focus Question 3**

How do we make and keep friends in kindergarten?

Vocabulary—English: *memories, expression, cooperate*

	Day 1	**Day 2**	**Day 3**
Interest Areas	Blocks: digital camera	Library: books about friendship	Library and Art: materials for adding to Sunshine Message Board
Question of the Day	Do you remember this day? (Display a photo from an event earlier in the school year.)	Do these two words rhyme? (Display two words with images.)	How do you like to show kindness to someone?
Large Group	Rhyme: Riddle Dee Dee **Discussion and Shared Writing:** Remembering the Beginning of the Year **Materials:** Mighty Minutes 04, "Riddle Dee Dee"; chart paper	Story: Listening Story **Discussion and Shared Writing:** How Do We Make Friends? **Materials:** Mighty Minutes 86, "Listening Story"; audio or video recorder	Song: "The Kids Go Marching In" **Discussion and Shared Writing:** Being Kind to Others **Materials:** Mighty Minutes 70, "The Kids Go Marching In"; chart paper
Read-Aloud	Selection of a book from the "Children's Books" list that focuses on the feelings of characters	*The Upside Down Boy* Book Discussion Card 42 (third read-aloud)	Reread the book from Day 1 that focuses on the feelings of characters.
Small Group	Option 1: Bookmaking Intentional Teaching Card LL04, "Bookmaking"; cardboard or card stock; paper; pencils, crayons, or markers; bookbinding supplies Option 2: Desktop Publishing Intentional Teaching Card LL02, "Desktop Publishing"; digital camera; computer; each child's word bank; printer; paper; bookbinding supplies	Option 1: Bookmaking Intentional Teaching Card LL04, "Bookmaking"; cardboard or card stock; paper; pencils, crayons, or markers; bookbinding supplies Option 2: Desktop Publishing Intentional Teaching Card LL02, "Desktop Publishing"; digital camera; computer; each child's word bank; printer; paper; bookbinding supplies	Option 1: Nursery Rhyme Count Intentional Teaching Card M13, "Nursery Rhyme Count"; cotton balls or white pompoms; green construction paper; numeral cards Option 2: Bounce & Count Intentional Teaching Card M18, "Bounce & Count"; a variety of balls that bounce
Mighty Minutes™	Mighty Minutes 26, "Echo Clapping"	Mighty Minutes 85, "Listen for Your Name"	Mighty Minutes 49, "A Tree My Size"

Spanish: *recuerdos, expresión, cooperar*

Day 4	Day 5	Make Time for...
Library: materials for making cards; Intentional Teaching Card SE19, "Friendship & Love Cards"	Music and Movement: recordings of music for dancing	**Outdoor Experiences** • Generate a list of children's favorite outdoor activities. Encourage children to choose a new activity each day to play.
What do you like to do with a friend?	Which of these is easier to do with a partner? (Display photos or props for different activities such as riding a bike, playing a board game, and brushing teeth.)	**Family Partnerships** • Invite family members to join the class for the end-of-year celebration next week.
Song: "Hello Friends" Discussion and Shared Writing: What Do We Do With Friends? Materials: Mighty Minutes 78, "Hello Friends"; chart paper	Rhyme: Humpty Dumpty Discussion and Shared Writing: Friendship Materials: Mighty Minutes 81, "Humpty Dumpty"; book from the Children's Book Collection; chart paper	
I Took the Moon for a Walk Book Discussion Card 43 (first read-aloud)	Selection of an information book from the "Children's Books" list	
Option 1: Story Problems Intentional Teaching Card M22, "Story Problems"; collection of manipulatives to be added and subtracted Option 2: More or Fewer Towers Intentional Teaching Card M59, "More or Fewer Towers"; interlocking cubes; more–fewer spinner; numeral–quantity cards or die	Option 1: Tallying Intentional Teaching Card M06, "Tallying"; clipboard; paper; pencils or crayons; chart from large group Option 2: Graphing Intentional Teaching Card M11, "Graphing"; large graph paper or lined chart paper; markers; stickers; charts from yesterday's and today's large group	
Mighty Minutes 16, "Nothing, Nothing, Something"	Mighty Minutes 10, "Words in Motion"	

Day 1 Focus Question 3

How do we make and keep friends in kindergarten?

Vocabulary

English: *memories*
Spanish: *recuerdos*
Question of the Day: Do you remember this day? (Display a photo from an event earlier in the school year.)

Large Group

Opening Routine

- Sing a welcome song and talk about who's here.

Rhyme: Riddle Dee Dee

- Use Mighty Minutes 04, "Riddle Dee Dee." Follow the guidance on the card.

Discussion and Shared Writing: Remembering the Beginning of the Year

- Review the question of the day. Invite children to recall the event and any details they remember.

- Say, "When we started our school year together, we talked about how to make friends. We've made many friends in this class."

- Invite children to think about their experiences making friends during the year. Introduce the word *memories* as what they remember when they think about what has happened before.

- Share a few of your own memories from earlier in the year. For example, "I remember when we first started school, many of you didn't know each other. Now you know everyone in the class, and you know about the things they like and don't like."

- Invite children to share something that they've learned about a classmate. Ask open-ended questions that prompt children to think about how they learned about their friends and classmates. For example, "Rabia said that she knows Casey loves to do puzzles but doesn't like to play board games. I wonder how she learned that about him?"

- Record children's responses.

Before transitioning to interest areas, invite children to work together to build a variety of block structures in the Block area during choice time.

Getting Ready for Kindergarten Focus Questions

Choice Time

As you interact with children in the interest areas, make time to do the following:

- Talk with children about the structures they build in the Block area. Ask, "What can you tell me about the structure you built?"

- Have conversations with individual children about what they like to do with their friends. Record their responses.

- Take photos of children's structures and the children who worked together to build them.

Read-Aloud

Choose a storybook from the "Children's Books" list found on pages 64–69 that focuses on the feelings of characters. See the accompanying guidance for ideas about sharing the book with children.

Small Group

If you have books that children made in the beginning of the year about what the class likes to do together, include them in the experience for children to explore and make comparisons as they create new books.

Option 1: Bookmaking

- Review Intentional Teaching Card LL04, "Bookmaking." Follow the guidance on the card.

- Invite children to create a book about things the class likes to do together at school.

Option 2: Desktop Publishing

- Review Intentional Teaching Card LL02, "Desktop Publishing." Follow the guidance on the card.

- Invite children to create a book about things the class likes to do together at school.

Mighty Minutes™

- Use Mighty Minutes 26, "Echo Clapping." Follow the guidance of the first bullet on the back of the card.

Large-Group Roundup

- Recall the day's events.

- Invite children who created block structures to talk about their creations and how they worked together during the experience.

The Creative Curriculum® for Preschool

37

Day 2 Focus Question 3

How do we make and keep friends in kindergarten?

Vocabulary
English: See Book Discussion Card 42, *The Upside Down Boy*, for words.
Question of the Day: Do these two words rhyme? (Display two words with images.)

Large Group

Opening Routine
- Sing a welcome song and talk about who's here.

Story: Listening Story
- Use Mighty Minutes 86, "Listening Story." Follow the guidance on the back of the card, and adapt the story to relate to a kindergarten experience.

Discussion and Shared Writing: How Do We Make Friends?
- Begin by sharing your thoughts about a special friend. For example, "My friend Dhruti is so special to me. She really cares about me and listens when I want to talk about a problem I have. We like to go to the movies together because we like the same movies. She makes me feel like I'm important to her."
- Ask children to pause for a moment and think about a special friend. Ask them to think about how that friend makes them feel and what they like about their friend. Invite them to share their thoughts. Create audio or video recordings of the experience or record their ideas on paper.
- Ask, "Can you remember how you met your friend? I remember that I met Dhruti when I joined a book club. We liked the same book. I was nervous about meeting new people, but I introduced myself so I could get to know the people there."
- Demonstrate how to introduce yourself, and invite the children to practice with the child next to them.

Before transitioning to interest areas, explain that there are books about friendship in the Library area. As children move between interest areas, encourage them to practice introducing themselves to others.

English-language learners
Use consistent gestures to illustrate the desired movements during transitions. Use these same gestures repeatedly throughout the day to help children connect the spoken words with the concept. For example, to signal that it is time to line up in front of you, you might hold up your hands with palms facing each other and raise and lower your arms as you say, "Line up."

Getting Ready for Kindergarten Focus Questions

Choice Time

As you interact with children in the interest areas, make time to do the following:

- Engage with children as they explore the books in the Library area. Ask open-ended questions that prompt them to think about the friendships in the books and their own friendships.

- Record their observations and thoughts about the books.

- Introduce yourself to children as you move around the room. Talk with children about their feelings on meeting new people.

Read-Aloud

Read *The Upside Down Boy*.

- Review Book Discussion Card 42, *The Upside Down Boy*. Follow the guidance for the third read-aloud.

Small Group

If you have books that children made in the beginning of the year about what the class likes to do together, include them in the experience for children to explore and make comparisons as they create new books.

Option 1: Bookmaking

- Review Intentional Teaching Card LL04, "Bookmaking." Follow the guidance on the card.

- Invite children to create a book about the things the class likes to do together at school.

Option 2: Desktop Publishing

- Review Intentional Teaching Card LL02, "Desktop Publishing." Follow the guidance on the card.

- Invite children to create a book about the things the class likes to do together at school.

Mighty Minutes™

- Review the question of the day.

- Use Mighty Minutes 85, "Listen for Your Name." Follow the guidance on the card.

- Repeat the game, and ask children to clap the syllables of the rhyming words.

- Ask children to help you sort the group by the number of syllables in each of their names, and then count the number of children in each group.

Large-Group Roundup

- Recall the day's events.

- Invite children to think about who they enjoyed playing with today. Take a moment again, and ask them to pause and think about a special friend.

The Creative Curriculum® for Preschool

Day 3 Focus Question 3

How do we make and keep friends in kindergarten?

Vocabulary

English: *expression*
Spanish: *expresión*
Question of the Day: How do you like to show kindness to someone?

Large Group

Opening Routine

- Sing a welcome song and talk about who's here.

Song: "The Kids Go Marching In"

- Use Mighty Minutes 70, "The Kids Go Marching In." Repeat the verses and ask the children to change the beginning letter of "doo dah" as they sing.

Discussion and Shared Writing: Being Kind to Others

- Tell children about a time when you showed kindness to a friend or a friend showed kindness to you. For example, "Remember last week when I didn't come to school because I was sick? My neighbor was very kind and brought me soup that he had made to help me feel better."

- Review the question of the day. Ask children to think about how they show others that they care. Give them plenty of time to think about your question.

- Record their responses. Talk about how each of the responses might make someone feel. For example, "Baylor said that she helps her baby brother pick up his toys. I wonder how that makes him feel."

- Encourage children to think of an idea for showing someone kindness today. Generate a list of ideas for children to refer to throughout the day.

Before transitioning to interest areas, explain that they can use materials in the Art or Library area to create messages to add to the Sunshine Message Board.

English-language learners
It is common for children to mix English and their home languages as they progress in their acquisition of English vocabulary. This is an effective way to participate and contribute to conversations. Restate what the child says, emphasizing the English vocabulary.

40

Getting Ready for Kindergarten Focus Questions

Choice Time

As you interact with children in the interest areas, make time to do the following:

- Talk with children about their creations for the Sunshine Message Board.

- Ask them open-ended questions about how they chose the person whom the message is for, what they're creating, and how they think it will make the recipient feel.

- Record their responses.

> **See Intentional Teaching Card SE21, "Sunshine Message Board," for guidance on sharing this experience with children.**

Read-Aloud

Reread the book from Day 1 that focuses on the feelings of the characters. Invite children to find examples in the story of people showing kindness to others.

Small Group

Option 1: Nursery Rhyme Count

- Review Intentional Teaching Card M13, "Nursery Rhyme Count." Follow the guidance on the card.

• Option 2: Bounce & Count

- Review Intentional Teaching Card M18, "Bounce & Count." Follow the guidance on the card.

Mighty Minutes™

- Use Mighty Minutes 49, "A Tree My Size." Follow the guidance on the card.

Large-Group Roundup

- Recall the day's events.
- Invite children to share the notes and drawings they added to the Sunshine Message Board.

- Explain that tomorrow they will have a chance to make cards for their special friends.

The Creative Curriculum® for Preschool

41

Day 4 Focus Question 3

How do we make and keep friends in kindergarten?

Vocabulary
English: See Book Discussion Card 43, *I Took the Moon for a Walk*, for words.
Question of the Day: What do you like to do with a friend?

Large Group

Opening Routine
- Sing a welcome song and talk about who's here.

Song: "Hello Friends"
- Use Mighty Minutes 78, "Hello Friends." Follow the guidance on the card.

Discussion and Shared Writing: What Do We Do With Friends?
- Point out examples of children playing together that you have noticed over the past few days. For example, "Yesterday, I saw Nadya and Thomas practicing how to jump rope together. I could see that they were really having fun."
- Review the question of the day. Invite children to name activities they like to do with their friends.
- Record their responses. If the same response is given more than once, tally the answers and count them together with children. Save the chart for tomorrow's large group time.

> See Intentional Teaching Card M06, "Tallying," for more information.

Before transitioning to interest areas, talk about the materials in the Library area and how children may use them to make a card for a friend.

Getting Ready for Kindergarten Focus Questions

Choice Time

As you interact with children in the interest areas, make time to do the following:

- Talk with children about their work in the Library area. Explain that the cards are an *expression* of how they feel. That means they show someone else what they're thinking and feeling.

- Record their dictation on their cards when asked.

- Invite children to talk about the friend for whom they are making the card.

> See Intentional Teaching Card SE19, "Friendship & Love Cards," for more information.

Read-Aloud

Read *I Took the Moon for a Walk*.

- Review Book Discussion Card 43, *I Took the Moon for a Walk*. Follow the guidance for the first read-aloud.

Small Group

Option 1: Story Problems

- Review Intentional Teaching Card M22, "Story Problems." Follow the guidance on the card.

Option 2: More or Fewer Towers

- Review Intentional Teaching Card M59, "More or Fewer Towers." Follow the guidance on the card.

Mighty Minutes™

- Use Mighty Minutes 16, "Nothing, Nothing, Something." Follow the guidance of the second bullet on the back of the card.

Large-Group Roundup

- Recall the day's events.
- Invite children who created cards to share them with the group.

The Creative Curriculum® for Preschool

43

Day 5 Focus Question 3

How do we make and keep friends in kindergarten?

Vocabulary

English: cooperate

Spanish: cooperar

Question of the Day: Which of these is easier to do with a partner? (Display photos or props for different activities, such as riding a bike, playing a board game, and brushing teeth.)

Large Group

Opening Routine

- Sing a welcome song and talk about who's here.

Rhyme: Humpty Dumpty

- Use Mighty Minutes 81, "Humpty Dumpty." Follow the guidance on the card.

Discussion and Shared Writing: Friendship

- Read a book that features friends from the Children's Book Collection, such as *The Adventures of Gary & Harry*, *Just Like Josh Gibson*, *Wemberly Worried*, or *Henny Penny*.

- Ask questions about the examples of friendship in the book. For example, "How do you know that Gary and Harry were friends? What did they do to show that they were friends? What did these friends like to do together?"

- Review the question of the day. Invite children to think about activities that are better with a friend. Record their responses.

- Explain that some activities such as building with blocks, cooking, or playing with a ball can be done alone, but they might be more fun with a friend. Talk about classroom activities that children enjoy doing together.

Before transitioning to interest areas, explain that children may want to listen to music and dance together in the Music and Movement area.

Getting Ready for Kindergarten Focus Questions

Choice Time

As you interact with children in the interest areas, make time to do the following:

- Observe how children choose music to listen to in the Music and Movement area.

- Call attention to examples of cooperation that you see. For example, "This looks like a fun dance party! I saw you *cooperated* to decide what music to listen to. That means you worked together."

English-language learners
Help children by modeling language for them. Provide language support as you encourage children to interact with each other. For example, say, "Ask Rose, 'May I please join you?'"

Read-Aloud

Choose a nonfiction book from the "Children's Books" list found on pages 64–69. See the accompanying guidance for additional ideas when sharing the book with children.

Small Group

Option 1: Tallying

- Review Intentional Teaching Card M06, "Tallying." Follow the guidance on the card, using the information gathered at large-group time.

Option 2: Graphing

- Review Intentional Teaching Card M11, "Graphing." Follow the guidance on the card.

- Include the charts from yesterday's and today's large-group times.

Mighty Minutes™

- Use Mighty Minutes 10, "Words in Motion." Follow the guidance of the second bullet on the back of the card. Call out the names of two children to perform the movements together.

Large-Group Roundup

- Recall the day's events.

- Invite children who danced together in the Music and Movement area to talk about their experience.

The Creative Curriculum® for Preschool

45

Reflecting and Celebrating

Reflecting and Celebrating

Unlike the celebration at the end of each study, this week is about more — it's about reflecting on and celebrating children's learning from the entire school year. It's about supporting children as they think back on what they've learned over the year and celebrate all they have accomplished. This is an important milestone in children's education. Plan a special way to celebrate children's learning and achievements and to reflect on the year together. Encourage children to assume as much responsibility as possible for planning the activities.

Here are some additional suggestions of ways to celebrate the end of the year together:

Art Gallery Show: Invite children to review their portfolios at the end of the year and encourage them to pick a few of their favorite pieces. Invite the children to help you turn the room (or a section of the room) into an art gallery. Check out some books from the library or look online with the children at pictures of famous art galleries so they can see the various ways that art is displayed. Invite families to visit the gallery as a special event, or take a tour with their child during drop-off or pick-up time. If your program is located near a college campus (many campuses have a small gallery for displaying student work) or a local art gallery, you may be able to use a part of the gallery space for an art show.

Child-Made Yearbooks: Print multiple copies of photos of the children from throughout the year. (You can use regular printer paper and even print the photos in black and white to save money.) Put the photos, collage materials, and book-making supplies in the Art area. Encourage children to create yearbooks with photos and decorations that reflect their year in the classroom. After the books are completed, children can sign each other's books by writing their names, putting a handprint in the book, adding a special sticker, or dictating a message for the teacher to record.

Reflect on the Year Through Poetry: As the children write poetry over the year as a class, in small groups, and individually, keep copies of the poems and their related illustrations or photographs. During the last days of school, write one final poem together about graduating and going to kindergarten. Compile all the poems into a book and provide copies to the children. They can take their copy home with them for a bit of summer reading.

Getting Ready for Kindergarten Reflecting and Celebrating

Study Stations: Host an event similar to the end-of-study events where children, families, and the school community are invited to celebrate children's learning. Set up stations with some of the hands-on investigations that children explored during the studies. For example: a ramp with different kinds of balls for the question, "Do all balls roll?"; craft sticks, glue, tape, and rubber bands to construct a building for the question, "What makes a building strong?"; and a water station with bar soap, powder soap, and liquid soap for the question, "How do we clean clothes?"

While guests participate in the stations, children can describe the stations, talk about the study topic, and explain what they discovered.

Welcome Pack: Encourage children to help you create a welcome package for incoming preK children. Invite children to include things that will help the next group be successful, for example: a copy of the daily schedule, a few artifacts from the studies they may explore, and copies of favorite books the class liked to read together.

Fun Family Event: Whether it is a family picnic, a big water play day, a field day with activity stations, building a bridge out of blocks which the children can cross ceremoniously, or a simple graduation ceremony, find a way to celebrate your school community with families.

Not every celebration idea will be appropriate for every school community. Take time to consider the children in your classroom, their families, and their home cultures, and pick a way to celebrate that is right for your school community.

The Creative Curriculum® for Preschool

49

AT A GLANCE # Reflecting and Celebrating

Vocabulary—English: *goal, accomplishment, reflect, look forward to*

	Day 1	Day 2	Day 3
Interest Areas	Library: personal journal for each child; variety of writing tools	Library: personal journal for each child; variety of writing tools	Art: materials for creating illustrations
Question of the Day	Which was your favorite study this year? (List the studies completed in your class.)	What are you proud of?	How old will you be when you go to kindergarten?
Large Group	**Movement:** Spatial Patterns **Discussion and Shared Writing:** What Did We Learn This Year? **Materials:** Mighty Minutes 38, "Spatial Patterns"; artifacts from the year's studies; audio or video recorder; chart paper	**Game:** My Name, Too! **Discussion and Shared Writing:** What Did We Learn This Year? **Materials:** Mighty Minutes 35, "My Name, Too!"; chart paper	**Rhyme:** Ticky Ricky **Discussion and Shared Writing:** Writing a Letter **Materials:** Mighty Minutes 12, "Ticky Ricky"; letter writing materials; chart paper
Read-Aloud	*I Took the Moon for a Walk* Book Discussion Card 43 (second read-aloud)	Selection of a fiction book from the "Children's Books" list	*I Took the Moon for a Walk* Book Discussion Card 43 (third read-aloud)
Small Group	**Option 1: Making Numerals** Intentional Teaching Card M41, "Making Numerals"; modeling dough or clay; numeral–quantity cards **Option 2: Math Collage** Intentional Teaching Card M78, "Math Collage"; construction paper; glue; collection of small collage materials, e.g., craft sticks, pom-poms, sequins, feathers, or other small materials related to the study topic; pencils or crayons; numeral–quantity cards	**Option 1: Letters, Letters, Letters** Intentional Teaching Card LL07, "Letters, Letters, Letters"; alphabet rubber stamps; colored ink pads; construction paper or magnetic letters and board **Option 2: Shaving Cream Letters** Intentional Teaching Card LL13, "Shaving Cream Letters"; shaving cream; art smocks	**Option 1: Morning, Noon, and Night** Intentional Teaching Card M60, "Morning, Noon, & Night"; magazines; scissors; chart paper; glue sticks; markers **Option 2: Which Container Holds More?** Intentional Teaching Card M32, "Which Container Holds More?"; sand table; various clear plastic containers; paper cup, measuring cup, or can; funnel
Mighty Minutes™	Mighty Minutes 08, "Clap the Missing Word"	Mighty Minutes 32, "Walk the Line"; masking tape or yarn; letter cards	Mighty Minutes 52, "Walk Around the Shapes"; shape cards

50

Spanish: *objetivo, logro, reflexionar, anhelar*

Day 4	Day 5	Make Time for...
All: displays of children's learning throughout the year	**All:** displays of children's learning throughout the year **Art:** materials for working on the mural	## Outdoor Experiences **Physical Fun** • Review Intentional Teaching Card P17, "Balance on a Beam." Follow the guidance on the card.
What was your favorite thing about preschool?	What is your favorite memory of our year together?	## Family Partnerships • Invite family members to join the class for the end-of-year celebration. • Invite older siblings, if possible, to share their personal kindergarten experiences.
Rhyme: A-Hunting We Will Go **Discussion and Shared Writing:** Planning Our Celebration **Materials:** Mighty Minutes 58, "A-Hunting We Will Go"; chart paper	**Game:** Simon Says **Discussion and Shared Writing:** Reflecting and Celebrating **Materials:** Mighty Minutes 13, "Simon Says"	
Selection of a fiction book from the "Children's Books" list	Books that children have made throughout the year	
Option 1: A Mural of Memories Intentional Teaching Card SE26, "Making a Mural"; materials for making a mural, e.g., smocks, paint, paintbrushes, etc. **Option 2: A Mural of Memories** Intentional Teaching Card SE26, "Making a Mural"; materials for making a mural, e.g., smocks, paint, paintbrushes, etc.; collection of photos and videos from earlier in the year	**Making a Snack to Share** *Come Cook With Me!* or an *Intentional Teaching Card™* for the recipe chosen yesterday; ingredients and materials for making recipe	
Mighty Minutes 82, "Let's Clean Up!"	Mighty Minutes 40, "Clap A Friend's Name"	

Day 1 — Reflecting and Celebrating

Vocabulary
English: *goal*; See Book Discussion Card 43, *I Took the Moon for a Walk*, for additional words
Spanish: *objetivo*
Question of the Day: Which was your favorite study this year? (List the studies completed in your class.)

Large Group

Opening Routine

- Sing a welcome song and talk about who's here.

Movement: Spatial Patterns

- Use Mighty Minutes 38, "Spatial Patterns." Follow the guidance on the back of the card.

Discussion and Shared Writing: What Did We Learn This Year?

- Review the question of the day.
- As you recall the different studies, encourage children to share what they remember most or what they liked the best. Record their responses.
- Share some of the creations and projects from earlier in the year. Invite children to look over the artifacts from the year and discuss them. If possible, create an audio or video recording of the experience.
- Say, "We have learned so much this year! We have lots of ideas and experiences to take with us to kindergarten. In kindergarten, we can learn new things, and we can learn more about the things we already know about."
- Encourage children to think of a learning goal for kindergarten, such as learning more about an important person in history or an interesting place to visit. Explain that *goal* can mean the points in a sports game, but it can also mean something that you decide you want to do, and then you work hard to do it, even if it takes a while.

Before transitioning to interest areas, explain that children can use their journals in the Library area to write down their goals for kindergarten.

Getting Ready for Kindergarten Reflecting and Celebrating

Choice Time

As you interact with children in the interest areas, make time to do the following:

- Talk with children about their learning goals. If they are having trouble thinking of goals, ask them to think about topics that interest them.

- Ask open-ended questions that prompt children to reflect on what they've learned and use what they've learned to create goals for kindergarten. For example, "I remember that you enjoyed learning about the muscles in your body when we did the Exercise study. What else could you learn about your body? Where could you look for this information?"

Read-Aloud

Read *I Took the Moon for a Walk*.

- Review Book Discussion Card 43, *I Took the Moon for a Walk*. Follow the guidance for the second read-aloud.

Small Group

Option 1: Making Numerals

- Review Intentional Teaching Card M41, "Making Numerals" Follow the guidance on the card.

Option 2: Math Collage

- Review Intentional Teaching Card M78, "Math Collage." Follow the guidance on the card.

Mighty Minutes™

- Use Mighty Minutes 08, "Clap the Missing Word." Follow the guidance on the card.

Large-Group Roundup

- Recall the day's events.
- Invite children who recorded their goals in their journals to share their experience.

The Creative Curriculum® for Preschool

53

Day 2 Reflecting and Celebrating

Vocabulary
English: *accomplishment*
Spanish: *logro*
Question of the Day: What are you proud of?

Large Group

Opening Routine

- Sing a welcome song and talk about who's here.

Game: My Name, Too!

- Use Mighty Minutes 35, "My Name, Too!" Follow the guidance on the card, including the variation on the back of the card where children make different movements.

Discussion and Shared Writing: What Did We Learn This Year?

- Say, "Yesterday, we thought about the studies that we did this year. But we didn't just learn about studies. Can you help me think of other things we learned?"

- Offer a suggestion of something you learned. For example, "This year I learned that one of my plants likes to drink lots of water and the other one doesn't."

- Prompt children to recall things they've learned, such as new rules, new self-care tasks, or new ways to use certain materials. Record their responses.

- Say, "When we talked about our learning goals yesterday, we were thinking about new information to find out about. Can we think of goals that we have for kindergarten that are about doing something new?"

- Record their responses. For example, "Rocky said he wants to tie his own shoes. That's a great goal, Rocky. With practice, you will learn to tie your shoes on your own."

Before transitioning to interest areas, explain that children can use their journals in the Library area to write down their goals for kindergarten.

Getting Ready for Kindergarten Reflecting and Celebrating

Choice Time

As you interact with children in the interest areas, make time to do the following:

- Review the question of the day. Ask open-ended questions that prompt children to reflect on what they've learned and how it makes them feel when they learn how to do something they couldn't do before. For example, "You were so proud when you figured out how to make your clay building stick together. That was a big *accomplishment* for you. That means you did something you were trying hard to do."

- Wonder aloud to help children think of new things they would like to accomplish. For example, "I wonder what else you could learn to do with the clay."

- Record your observations as children add to their journals.

Read-Aloud

Choose a storybook from the "Children's Books" list found on pages 64–69. See the accompanying guidance for ideas about sharing the book with children.

English-language learners
Using books with simple illustrations that provide visual cues about the meaning of the narrative helps children comprehend the content.

Small Group

Option 1: Letters, Letters, Letters

- Review Intentional Teaching Card LL07, "Letters, Letters, Letters." Follow the guidance on the card.

Option 2: Shaving Cream Letters

- Review Intentional Teaching Card LL13, "Shaving Cream Letters." Follow the guidance on the card.

Mighty Minutes™

- Use Mighty Minutes 32, "Walk the Line." Follow the guidance on the card.

Large-Group Roundup

- Recall the day's events.

- Review what the children have learned during the year. Encourage them to congratulate each other on their accomplishments.

The Creative Curriculum® for Preschool

55

Day 3 — Reflecting and Celebrating

Vocabulary
English: See Book Discussion Card 43, *I Took the Moon for a Walk*, for words.
Question of the Day: How old will you be when you go to kindergarten?

Large Group

Opening Routine
- Sing a welcome song and talk about who's here.

Rhyme: Ticky Ricky
- Use Mighty Minutes 12, "Ticky Ricky." Follow the guidance on the card.

Discussion and Shared Writing: Writing a Letter
- Review the question of the day. Tally the responses and share the results with the group. Talk about how old children were when they began the current school year.
- Say, "You were younger when you first came to this class. It was something new for you and maybe some of you felt nervous in the beginning. You had to learn new things like where to put your things, what do to do during morning meeting, and where our classroom materials belong."
- Explain that, as a group, you will write a letter to share with the children who will be in this class next year. Ask children to think about what they might want to include in the letter that would help someone who is new to the class.
- Record their responses.
- Together as a group, write the letter and include the children's responses.
- Let children know that you will share this letter with families when you send a welcome letter before the next school year.

Before transitioning to interest areas, explain that children will have a chance to help add illustrations to the letter in the Art area during choice time.

Getting Ready for Kindergarten Reflecting and Celebrating

Choice Time

As you interact with children in the interest areas, make time to do the following:

- Talk with children as they think about what they might like to include in their illustrations.

- Observe and ask questions about their creations. Encourage them to think back to some of their experiences earlier in the year.

- Record their thoughts and ideas.

Read-Aloud

Read *I Took the Moon for a Walk*.

Review Book Discussion Card 43, *I Took the Moon for a Walk*. Follow the guidance for the third read-aloud.

Small Group

Option 1: Morning, Noon, and Night

- Review Intentional Teaching Card M60, "Morning, Noon, and Night." Follow the guidance on the card.

Option 2: Which Container Holds More?

- Review Intentional Teaching Card M32, "Which Container Holds More?" Follow the guidance on the card.

Mighty Minutes™

- Use Mighty Minutes 52, "Walk Around the Shapes." Follow the guidance on the card.

Large-Group Roundup

- Recall the day's events.

- Invite children who illustrated the letter to share their ideas and creations.

- Explain that tomorrow they will begin planning their end-of-year celebration.

The Creative Curriculum® for Preschool

57

Day 4 | Reflecting and Celebrating

Vocabulary

English: *reflect*
Spanish: *reflexionar*
Question of the Day: What was your favorite thing about preschool?

Large Group

Opening Routine

- Sing a welcome song and talk about who's here.

Rhyme: A-Hunting We Will Go

- Use Mighty Minutes 58, "A-Hunting We Will Go." Follow the guidance on the card.

Discussion and Shared Writing: Planning Our Celebration

- Explain, "We've spent this week taking the time to *reflect* on everything we've accomplished this year. Reflect means to think carefully about. Now it's time to celebrate our hard work! Tomorrow our families and friends will join us in our celebration."

- Ask, "What snack should we make tomorrow for our visitors?" Show the children a few recipe choices and then take a vote. Choose the recipe that has the most votes.

- Encourage children to think about what they want to share with the visitors tomorrow. Remind them that they can think back over the whole year and not just one study.

- Record their responses, and write down what artifacts and creations they want to share.

Before transitioning to interest areas, tell children that you will help them gather the items from the list to create displays for family and friends to see at tomorrow's celebration.

Getting Ready for Kindergarten Reflecting and Celebrating

Choice Time

As you interact with children in the interest areas, make time to do the following:

- Help them decide what materials they would like to share at the celebration.

- Talk with children about the difference between this celebration and the celebrations at the end of each study.

> **Be mindful of children who are especially anxious about the upcoming transition. Listen to their fears and worries and offer them strategies to help them cope with their anxiety.**

Read-Aloud

Choose a storybook from the "Children's Books" list found on pages 64–69. See the accompanying guidance for additional ideas when sharing the book with children.

Small Group

Option 1: A Mural of Memories

- Review the question of the day. Invite children to make a mural of their favorite school memories.

- Review Intentional Teaching Card SE26, "Making a Mural."

- Follow the guidance on the card.

Option 2: A Mural of Memories

- Review the question of the day. Invite children to make a mural of their favorite school memories.

- Review Intentional Teaching Card SE26, "Making a Mural."

- Follow the guidance on the card. Before beginning, show children a collection of photos and videos from earlier in the year that they can think about as they create their mural.

English-language learners
When interacting with English-language learners, you may notice that some children repeat English words or phrases. These children are practicing using the language—they are exploring the pronunciation, intonation, grammar, and meanings of words. Rephrase their answers and acknowledge their efforts.

Mighty Minutes™

- Use Mighty Minutes 20, "Let's Clean Up!" Follow the guidance on the card.

Large-Group Roundup

- Recall the day's events.

- Remind the children that they will be taking part in a special celebration tomorrow.

The Creative Curriculum® for Preschool

59

Day 5 | Reflecting and Celebrating

Vocabulary
English: : look forward to
Spanish: anhelar
Question of the Day: What is your favorite memory from our year together?

Large Group

Opening Routine
- Sing a welcome song and talk about who's here.

Game: Simon Says
- Use Mighty Minutes 13, "Simon Says." Follow the guidance on the card.
- Invite children to lead the activity and to take turns calling on other children to lead.

Discussion and Shared Writing: Reflecting and Celebrating
- Welcome families to the celebration.
- Explain that this is the time of year when we reflect on our wonderful time together in preschool and *look forward to* going to kindergarten.
- Review the question of the day. Share a couple of your favorite memories from the year.
- Explain to families that children have gathered materials from the entire year and are excited to share what they've learned.
- Briefly review the documentation from the first focus question about all of the different feelings children might have about going to kindergarten. Encourage children to share their ideas.
- Invite any older siblings or other family members to talk about their kindergarten experiences.

Before transitioning to interest areas, talk about the displays of children's learning that you've set up around the room.

60

Getting Ready for Kindergarten Reflecting and Celebrating

Choice Time

As you interact with children in the interest areas, make time to do the following:

- Encourage children to explain to the visitors what they've learned during the year. Support visitors to ask questions that prompt the children to talk about what they've learned.

- Invite children to share their kindergarten goals with their families and friends.

- Provide art materials for children and their visitors to continue to add to the mural from yesterday.

Read-Aloud

Gather a collection of books that the children have made during the school year. Choose a few to read together.

As you read, encourage children to reflect on the year by talking about the ideas and illustrations they added to the books.

Small Group

Making a Snack to Share

- Remind children of the recipe that was chosen yesterday to make for today's celebration.

- Using *Come Cook With Me!* or an *Intentional Teaching Card™*, support children and families to work together and make the snack.

- Talk about the ingredients used and the steps to make the recipe.

- Invite everyone to enjoy the snack together and talk about how it was made.

Mighty Minutes™

- Use Mighty Minutes 40, "Clap a Friend's Name" Follow the guidance on the card.

Large-Group Roundup

- Recall the day's events.

- Look at the mural you created over the last couple of days. Invite children to talk about their contributions.

The Creative Curriculum® for Preschool

61

Resources

Getting Ready for Kindergarten Resources

Children's Books

In addition to the children's books specifically used in this *Teaching Guide*, you may wish to supplement daily activities and interest areas with some of the listed children's books.

The following books are **about going to school:**

The Kissing Hand (Audrey Penn) Chester Raccoon prepares for his first "day" of school. After reading, talk with children about how Chester's mother kisses his hand to help him feel safe and loved on his first day. Invite children to share their family rituals that make them feel loved.

Wemberly Worried (Kevin Henkes) Wemberly worries about everything, especially the first day of school. Refer to the related Book Discussion Card 20 for ideas on using the book to support children's social–emotional development.

Countdown to Kindergarten (Alison McGhee) This book explores a child's feelings about the unknown of going to kindergarten and the perception of insurmountable challenges. After reading this book, begin a conversation about children's worries about new rules in kindergarten.

I Am Too Absolutely Small for School (Lauren Child) Lola is nervous about school, until her big brother Charlie encourages her and reassures her that her invisible friend can attend with her. After reading, invite children to talk about people they know who will also be attending their new school.

Mom, It's My First Day of Kindergarten (Hyewon Yum) Usually, it's the child who is anxious about the first day of school, but in this charming book, the nervous one is Mom! After reading, invite children to talk about how children and their families can support each other during the upcoming transition.

How Will I Get to School This Year? (Jerry Pallotta) In this story, a child considers all the different ways she can get to school. As you read, occasionally pause before turning the page, and invite children to predict the next idea. After reading, invite children to talk about all the different ways—real and imaginary—to get to school.

Look Out Kindergarten, Here I Come! (Nancy Carlson) Henry is excited to start kindergarten, but as the day approaches, he starts to lose a bit of confidence. Share this book when talking with children about what they can expect from their own kindergarten experiences. After reading, make connections between what Henry does in kindergarten and what the children will do.

Annabelle Swift, Kindergartner (Amy Schwartz) In this delightful book, Annabelle Swift, kindergartner, receives advice for her first day of kindergarten from Lucy, her older sister. Although some of Lucy's lessons are a bit unusual, which children will delight in, they ultimately help Annabelle save the day. As you read, invite children to share what they think of Lucy's lessons to Annabelle and what they think Annabelle is feeling at different points in the story. After reading, ask children what their older siblings have shared with them about going to kindergarten.

64

Children's Books

Additional **Spanish-language or bilingual** books for this category include the following:

¡Qué nervios! El primer dia de escuela (Julie Danneberg) Sarah Jane is so nervous about school, she doesn't want to go at all. As you read, invite children to describe how Sarah Jane feels and predict what will happen when she goes to school.

Un beso en mi mano (Audrey Penn) Chester Raccoon prepares for his first "day" of school. After reading, talk with children about how Chester's mother kisses his hand to help him feel safe and loved on his first day. Invite children to share their family rituals that make them feel loved.

Prudencia se preocupa (Kevin Henkes) Wemberly worries about everything, especially the first day of school. Refer to the related Book Discussion Card 20 for ideas on using the book to support children's social–emotional development.

Max va a la escuela (Adria F. Klein) In this book about a boy who loves to read, Max learns about all the wonderful things he can do at school and in the library. If possible, visit a nearby elementary school library, and ask the librarian to explain the process for borrowing and returning books.

¡Prepárate, kindergarten! ¡Allá voy! (Nancy Carlson) Henry is excited to start kindergarten, but as the day approaches, he starts to lose a bit of confidence. Share this book when talking with children about what they can expect from their own kindergarten experiences. After reading, make connections between what Henry does in kindergarten and what they will do.

David va al colegio (David Shannon and Teresa Mlawer) What will happen when David brings his unmistakable personality to a new setting—school? This book with the popular character, David, illustrates the importance of following classroom rules. As you read, invite children to predict what David will do next and what his teacher will say. After reading this book, revisit the classroom rules, and ask children to create a list of rules that would help David at school.

The following books feature **poetry:**

The Twelve Days of Kindergarten: A Counting Book (Deborah Lee Rose) Children are introduced to kindergarten through this sweet counting poem set to the tune of "The Twelve Days of Christmas." As you sing the song, pause occasionally to invite children to offer the number and the item being counted.

Hi, Koo! A Year of Seasons (Jon J. Muth) Introduce children to the beautiful style of poetry called haiku. After reading the story, invite children to count the number of syllables for each line, encouraging them to notice the pattern for each poem. Use this book with the children to create haiku poems using descriptive words that follow the 5-7-5 syllable pattern.

I Carry Your Heart With Me (e.e. cummings) Children are introduced to the poetry of e.e. cummings through this adaptation of one of his most popular poems. Ask children to share the ways in which their family members show their love. Point out the collage style of the illustrations, and encourage children to create a similar mixed-media collage using materials found in the Art area.

Getting Ready for Kindergarten Resources

Children's Books

Additional **Spanish-language or bilingual** books for this category include the following:

Taquititán de poemas (Ana Palmero Cáceres) In this Spanish poetry collection by Venezuela's most popular poets, lovely short poems celebrate nature and the wonder of childhood. As you read, invite children to notice the descriptive and figurative language and rhymes and rhythm in the poems. Point out that some poems rhyme and some do not. After reading, invite children to use descriptive words to describe everyday events and objects to create and illustrate their own poem.

Poems to Dream Together/Poemas para soñar juntos (Franciso Alarcon) This colorful poetry book introduces children to poetry in English and in Spanish. Explain that some poems, like those in this book, use descriptive language rather than rhyming words. Ask children to help you generate a descriptive poem and illustrate it in the style of the book. See Intentional Teaching Card LL27, "Writing Poems," for further guidance.

Mamá Goose: A Latino Nursery Treasury (Alma Flor Ada and F. Isabel Campoy) This beautiful collection of poetry features songs and rhymes from all over the world. As you read, invite children to repeat the words in the rhymes and talk about the illustrations.

The following are **friendship** books:

The Paper Bag Princess (Robert N. Munsch) What happens when a princess' prince is taken away by a ferocious dragon? Will Princess Elizabeth save the day and marry Prince Ronald? Use the related Book Discussion Card 08 as you read this book. After reading, review the Supporting Social–Emotional Development section of the card and discuss the way Ronald reacts to Elizabeth's appearance after rescuing him. Invite children to share ideas for getting to know and become friends with new people.

The Adventures of Gary & Harry (Lisa Matsumoto) Gary and Harry are the best of friends, exploring their ocean home. As you read, point out that Gary and Harry are different kinds of turtles with different interests. Invite children to talk about how friends don't always have to like and do the same things as each other. Refer to Book Discussion Card 09 as you read.

Best Best Friends (Margaret Chodos-Irvine) This book explores the ups and downs of the relationship between two best friends. Talk with children about the conflicts and resolutions that occur in the story. Invite them to relate the book to their own experiences with friends.

The Farmer and the Clown (Marla Frazee) This wordless book beautifully illustrates the unlikely friendship between a farmer and a clown. As you read, invite children to describe the illustrations and take part in the telling of the story.

Flora and the Penguin (Molly Idle) This fun wordless book takes a look at a girl named Flora and the adventures she has with her new penguin friend. Share this book with children more than once, and give them an opportunity to read the story to you.

Getting Ready for Kindergarten Resources

Children's Books

Additional **Spanish-language or bilingual** books for this category include the following:

La princesa vestida con una bolsa de papel (Robert N. Munsch) What happens when a princess' prince is taken away by a ferocious dragon? Will Princess Elizabeth save the day and marry Prince Ronald? Use the related Book Discussion Card 08 as you read this book. After reading, review the Supporting Social–Emotional Development section of the card and discuss the way Ronald reacts to Elizabeth's appearance after rescuing him. Invite children to share ideas for getting to know and become friends with new people.

Las aventuras de Gary y Harry (Lisa Matsumoto) Gary and Harry are the best of friends, exploring their ocean home. As you read, point out that Gary and Harry are different kinds of turtles with different interests. Invite children to talk about how friends don't always have to like and do the same things as each other. Refer to Book Discussion Card 09 as you read.

Marisol McDonald Doesn't Match/ Marisol McDonald No Combina (Monica Brown) This book features Marisol, an independent girl who loves her uniqueness. As you read, invite children to share what is unique about them and how they share their ideas and interests with their friends.

The following are books about **families**:

Kevin and His Dad (Irene Smalls) In this lovely book, Kevin and his father work together to complete chores around the house before going out to play and watch a movie. As you read, point out the rhyming words and sounds in the text and occasionally pause for children to fill in the repeating words. After reading the story, invite children to talk about their favorite people, and describe what they like to do with their family members and friends.

Love Is a Family (Roma Downey) Lily is worried that she and her mother will be the weirdest family at Family Fun Night. What will happen when she meets the other families? After reading this sweet story, invite children to talk about what Lily's mother says to comfort her, and discuss the different kinds of families of the children in the story.

I Love Saturdays y Domingos (Alma Flor Ada) This bilingual book tells the story of a child who celebrates both sides of her family. She enjoys the time she spends with her grandparents on the weekends. After reading, invite children to share the things they like to do with their families. Encourage them to write letters or draw pictures for their family members.

Dear Primo: A Letter to My Cousin (Duncan Tonatiuh) Charlie and Carlitos are cousins who live in different countries. They love to write letters to each other to share and compare their daily experiences, such as going to school and playing outside. Lead a discussion with children about the different ways to stay in touch with family and friends who live far away.

The Creative Curriculum® for Preschool

Getting Ready for Kindergarten Resources

Children's Books

Additional **Spanish-language or bilingual** books for this category include the following:

I Love Saturdays y Domingos (Alma Flor Ada) This bilingual book tells the story of a child who celebrates both sides of her family. She enjoys the time she spends with her grandparents on the weekends. After reading, invite children to share the things they like to do with their families. Encourage them to write letters or draw pictures for their family members.

Kevin y su papá (Irene Smalls) In this lovely book, Kevin and his father work together to complete chores around the house, before going out to play and watch a movie. As you read, point out the rhyming words and sounds in the text and occasionally pause for children to fill in the repeating words. After reading the story, invite children to talk about their favorite people, and describe what they like to do with their family members and friends.

El amor es la familia (Roma Downey) Lily is worried that she and her mother will be the weirdest family at Family Fun Night. What will happen when she meets the other families? After reading this sweet story, invite children to talk about what Lily's mother says to comfort her, and discuss the different kinds of families of the children in the story.

The following books are **informational, nonfiction** books:

It's Back to School We Go! First Day Stories From Around The World (Ellen Jackson) In this beautifully-illustrated book, children from around the world share their stories about what school is like on the first day. Invite children to describe what these stories have in common. Record their answers, and ask them to predict what they think their first day in kindergarten might be like.

Mailing May (Michael O. Tunnell) In this beautifully illustrated, fictionalized story of a real event, Charlotte May is sent by her parents to visit her grandmother, by mail! Readers learn about life in 1914 and the new parcel post regulations of the day. Use this book to talk about how May might have felt on her journey. Invite children to notice how their world is different or similar to May's world.

Punched Paper (Dani Sneed and Josie Fonseca) In this book, real photos show children preparing punched paper (called papél picado in Spanish) decorations for a classroom party. Invite children to follow the instructions in the book to make their own punched paper decorations for the end-of-the-year celebration.

Additional **Spanish-language or bilingual** books for this category include the following:

Así vamos a la escuela (Edith Baer) Find out how children from all around the world get to school in this sweet book. As you read, invite children to point out the similarities and differences between the different modes of transportation. After reading this book, create a chart for the different ways the children in the class get to school. Next, invite children to think of other creative ways they could get to school, and vote on their favorite!

Children's Books

The following are books about **feelings**:

Lilly's Purple Plastic Purse (Kevin Henkes) In this book, Lilly deals with the strong emotion of anger when her teacher takes away her prized possessions. Invite children to think of different ways Lilly could have reacted when she got angry. Encourage children to share a time when they were angry and how they expressed their feelings.

What If…? (Anthony Browne) Joe is excited about going to a big party. But then he starts to get nervous, asking, " What if?" He worries, " Will I have fun? Will I like the games and the people at the party?" After reading, ask children to join you in a shared writing experience as you talk about the children's worries and how they work through their feelings. Encourage them to think about who helps them when they're worried.

Rainstorm (Barbara Lehman) This wordless book starts with the lonely feeling of being home in a rainstorm with no one to play with and ends with an exciting adventure. Talk with children about feelings such as loneliness, anxiousness, and nervousness. Encourage children to relate the story to their own experiences.

Glad Monster, Sad Monster (Ed Emberley) This book explores lots of feelings that children experience and gives a name to them. Share this book with children when talking about how they feel about going to kindergarten. Encourage them to make their own monster masks to reflect their feelings.

Additional **Spanish-language or bilingual** books for this category include the following:

Monstruo Triste, Monstruo Feliz (Anne Miranda) This book explores lots of feelings that children experience and gives a name to them. Share this book with children when talking about how they feel about going to kindergarten. Encourage them to make their own monster masks to reflect their feelings.

Así me siento yo (Janan Cain) This colorful rhyming book uses descriptive words to illustrate strong emotions. As you read, pause before starting to describe the new emotion. Invite children to guess how the child in the story feels based on facial expressions and gestures. After reading, begin a conversation about different ways to express and manage strong emotions. Create a photo book with children demonstrating strong emotions.

Getting Ready for Kindergarten Resources

Teacher Resources

The teacher resources provide you with additional information and ideas for enhancing and extending the study topic.

Kindergarten Readiness
(Nancy L. Cappelloni) This book is a great reference of concepts related to kindergarten readiness. Review this book for ideas to support families during the transition and to address all areas of development and learning for children as they move up to kindergarten, and for general transition practices.

Ready for Kindergarten!:
From Recognizing Colors to Making Friends, Your Essential Guide to Kindergarten Prep (Deborah J. Stewart) This handbook for families offers ideas for play-based activities to help prepare children for a smooth transition to kindergarten.

Getting Ready for Kindergarten Resources

Weekly Planning Form

Week of: _____

Teacher: _____

Study: _____

	Monday	Tuesday	Wednesday	Thursday	Friday
Interest Areas					
Large Group					
Read-Aloud					
Small Group					

Outdoor Experiences:

Family Partnerships:

Wow! Experiences:

©2015 Teaching Strategies, LLC, Bethesda, MD; www.TeachingStrategies.com
Permission is granted to duplicate the material on this page for use in programs implementing *The Creative Curriculum® for Preschool.*

Weekly Planning Form, continued

"To Do" List:

Reflecting on the week:

Individual Child Planning

Getting Ready for Kindergarten Resources

©2015 Teaching Strategies, LLC, Bethesda, MD; www.TeachingStrategies.com
Permission is granted to duplicate the material on this page for use in programs implementing *The Creative Curriculum® for Preschool.*